Our progressive, cutting edge training program is nationally recognized in the training arena, and is a model to others.

Local 8 family marching in the Labor Day Parade in Toledo, 2000.

"It is the Local 8 members that exude the solidarity and work ethic of the union, and it is their duty to uphold these ideals."

Local 8 pioneers, 1935.
Standing (l-r) Arthur Sampsell, unknown, Frank Fischer (President 1941-1964), Clarence "Whitey" Bremer (Business Manager 1952-1960), Seated: Oliver Myers (Business Manager 1914-1952).

Preeter Electric 1952
IBEW Bowling Tournament Champs.

TOLEDO

Our Life, Our Times, Our Town

1800s – 1950 Toledo, Ohio

John R. Husman
Editor

Kelly J. Norwood
Project Manager

Sara E. Welborn
Creative Director/Graphic Designer

THE BLADE
toledoblade.com®

COVER PHOTOGRAPH.

St. Clair Street, looking south from Adams Street circa 1941.

The Adams and St. Clair street intersection was alive with retail and entertainment activity in 1941. The S.S. Kresge "5 and 10" is at the right in this photograph. Businesses seen, moving away from the camera, on St Clair Street include; Williams Grill, Pantheon Theater, Ziegler's Shoe Store, Manhattan Restaurant, Granada Theater, Tick Tock Milk Bar and, at the corner of Madison Avenue, the Produce Exchange. Opposite the Produce Exchange on Madison is The Ohio Building. The building to the right of the Produce exchange is the Edison Building at the corner of Madison Avenue and Superior Street. The 2005 photograph reveals changes. The prominent buildings remain, and are in use, but others have been replaced by parking facilities. Downtown Toledo is no longer a retail center, but it is a workplace and many people use private transportation for their daily commute.

The Blade 2005

Toledo-Lucas County Public Library circa 1941

Published by The Blade
A Block Communications Company
541 North Superior Street
Toledo OH 43660
Printed in the United States of America

For General Information, Customer Service, and Orders Contact:
Telephone   419.724.6545
                 800.245.3317
FAX   419.724.6080
E-Mail   historybook@toledoblade.com

FOREWORD

This book of historical photos from Toledo's past is truly a work of art. It is unique in that all the photos have been submitted by current and former residents of the Glass City. The pictures were found in old trunks, scrapbooks, or the bedside table of somebody's distant relative.

Collectively, they tell the pictorial history of the turn of the century in one of Ohio's largest cities. They show life in a way not seen until the master hand of editor, John Husman, put them all together in a book meant to become a keepsake for generations to come.

Now, one can see and learn about wooden sidewalks, horse-drawn grocery wagons, boats on a canal and, great-great-grandma dressed in all her flowing finery. There are photos of buildings still here and buildings never to be seen again, except in this collection.

The response of photo submissions from The Blade readers has been overwhelming. More than 800 photographs have been submitted and Editor John R. Husman has selected 300 to appear in volume one. Our plans are to publish two more volumes in the years ahead.

It is probably a good idea to purchase one of these books for every member of your family or for friends and neighbors because these photos will never be reproduced again. Each submitted picture will be returned to their respective owners who will return them to the places where they have been resting for many years.

Enjoy the special treat of looking through the pages in volume one of *The Blade's TOLEDO: Our Life, Our Times, Our Town*. It is truly a great book published by one of America's great newspapers!

Joseph H. Zerbey, IV
Vice President & General Manager
The Blade

EDITOR'S NOTE

This view of Toledo history is only possible because of the generosity of our readers who have graciously entrusted us with their photographs of people at home, at work, and at play and scenes of Toledo and its surrounding communities. We have assembled these into a volume that is unique in format and features photographs, most of which have not previously been published.

We have presented each photograph with a short caption that tells its story. In most cases, we have relied upon the information shared with us by the donor for this purpose. For some, we have provided supplemental research and have included a bibliography of the sources consulted. An index of all the historical surnames mentioned in the captions is included along with a listing of all those who contributed photographs to this volume. The photographs are old, sometimes have not been well cared for, or have even been abused. For the most part, we present them as they came to us, with tears, folds and other damage. We consider these imperfections to be a part of the pictures themselves.

Many people contributed to this publication. Most important among these are the readers who have shared their personal treasures. Jim Marshall, Manager of The Toledo-Lucas County Public Library, Local History and Genealogy Department, and Mary Mackzum, Head Librarian for The Blade provided invaluable assistance. Jane Bryan Welborn did double-duty as a proof reader and caption writer. Donna Christian, Ann Hurley and Greg Miller provided a number of research "miracles." Fred Folger, educator and historian extraordinaire, was tireless as he assisted with proofreading, fact-checking, and guidance. Joe Zerbey, Vice President & General Manager of The Blade, provided the vision to embark on the project and also the resources and freedom to accomplish it. Many others have helped along the way. Taken in total, their contribution is a major one. They are: Mark Woodruff, Laura Voelz, Louis Visi, Harry Villalon, Fred Temby, Yolanda Danyi Szuch, Molly Stebli, Isabel Sloan, Tammy Ragan, Nathan Parsons, Terri Parker, Bob Nicholas, Mike Nelson, Kathy Mortensen, Ron Mauter, Irene Martin, Mike Lora, Ken Levin, Pauline Kynard, Neilah Kirchner, Rod Kinn, Laura King, Jack Kerin, Kim Johns, Sandy Husman, Ann Hurley, Patti Hoag, Paul Herzig, Karen Heebsh, Nancy Hawkins, Alexis Hager, Pam Griesinger, Dan Gallerno, Doug Dinnebeil, Ken Dickson, Joseph Coyle, Edrene Cole and Tim Boaden. Finally, thanks are due to the people who did the real work of producing this volume. The staff that actually produced the book is small, dedicated, professional and hard-working. It has been my pleasure to work with Kelly J. Norwood, the Project Manager, and Sara E. Welborn, the book's Creative Director/Graphic Designer. Hats off and thank you, Kelly and Sara! I apologize to any that I may have missed. I hope that you enjoy what our work has produced.

John R. Husman
Editor

A WELL-TRAVELED PHOTOGRAPH.

The prominent building in this 1861 photograph is a new Toledo fire station. The station, on the west side of Cherry Street, between Superior and Huron streets, housed Engine and Hose Company Number 1. The large apparatus in front of the open door is a hand-drawn, steam driven water pumper (steamer). Operationally, firefighting was brutally tiring work in 1861. The steamer, here, is about to be pulled by an eight-man team through the mud streets to the site of the fire. A bugler is poised to sound the signal for departure. A hose cart will also be dispatched to the scene. Once there, the steamer pumps water from a local water source, commonly a stream, pond or cistern. Toledo's Fire Department was all-volunteer until 1867.

This is a remarkable photograph and the story of its journey to this page is remarkable as well. Central to that story is Toledoan William P. Scott. Scott had enlisted as a Sergeant in Company K of the 25th Ohio Volunteer Infantry. His initial Civil War service was at Cheat Mountain, Virginia. Prior to his departure he was very much interested in Toledo's new engine house. According to John M. Killits', Toledo and Lucas County Ohio, (1923), "When the building was completed, a pic-

Dennis M. Keesee collection

ture of it, with the company, engine and hose cart in front, was taken and sent to Lieutenant Scott [ed. Sergeant] at Cheat Mountain, Virginia, where he received it in August, 1861. He carried the picture with him during the remainder of his service and upon his return used to tell how homesick he would get when he looked at it."

Scott's Civil War service was long, just days short of five years. Along the way he was promoted to First Sergeant, 2nd Lieutenant, 1st Lieutenant and finally to Captain. In 1864, he was transferred to his regiment's Company A. His units were involved in many actions and major battles including those at Bull Run, Gettysburg and Chancellorsville. Scott was twice wounded in action, at Chancellorsville and later, at Statesburg, South Carolina. According to his obituary, he was granted furlough during the latter part of the war in order to return to Toledo to recruit replacements for his depleted company. While at home, he mar-

ried, leaving his bride one hour after the ceremony, and not seeing her again for two years. After serving with occupation forces he, and this photograph, returned home in June of 1866.

Reunited with his wife, Catherine, they reared a family in a home he built at 934 Broadway. Toledo's first full-time police force was formed in 1867, and William Scott was made Sergeant. He spent the rest of his life serving as a Toledo police officer in various capacities, including Chief of Police, two times.

William P. Scott died in 1898, and was buried in Forest Cemetery. After his death, the photograph was enlarged by his, daughter, Nellie Young, who hung it in her parlor. It has been retained by Captain William P. Scott's descendants until it was recently donated to the Toledo Firefighter's Museum by Julie Munson, a great-great-granddaughter. *Submitted by the Toledo Firefighters Museum.*

DAUGHTER'S DAY AT WORK.

Toledo Firefighter, Oscar Gundlack, and his daughter, Mayme, sit on Hook and Ladder Company Number 7's horse-drawn, four-wheel hose wagon. The company's station was located at Bancroft Street and Franklin Avenue and was in operation from 1873 to 1968 — a long life of 95 years. The photograph was taken in 1898, as determined from examination of Mr. Gundlach's service record. Although first appointed as a fire-fighter on August 12, 1882, he was not assigned to Station Number 7 until 1898. He retired from the force as a Ladderman on August 1, 1898. A new station was built on this site and opened October 31, 1969. *Submitted by Mark Walczak.*

2

Michael Martin Goulden

STRIP MALL.

This circa 1872 photograph depicts several businesses in close proximity on the south side of Dorr Street between Heston Street and Junction Avenue. To the right is D. Rosenfeld's dry goods and clothing store. A dentist, by the name of Ross, had hung a sign between the buildings. The building closest to the camera was occupied by Michael Martin Goulden's Meat Market. Goulden offered fresh, dried, and smoked meats, fish, boiled ham, bologna, summer sausage, and bacon. He also advertised vegetables, bread, and dairy products, such as milk, eggs and butter. Goulden was born in Ireland and married Kate McDermott in 1858. He was a Civil War veteran, as well as a former member of Toledo City Council. At the time of this picture, he was Treasurer of Adams Township. He started in the grocery business in 1866 with a store at St. Clair and Layfayette streets and moved to this Dorr Street location in 1868. The business proved to be lasting. He was succeeded by his sons, George and Tom, in 1895 and the family continued the business at other locations past 1950. *Submitted by Mary Pat Carter Reifsnider, great-granddaughter of Michael and Kate Goulden.*

Toledo-Lucas County Public Library 1838-1950

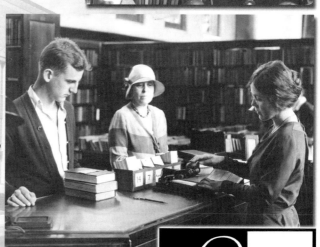

Tracing its origins to 1838, one year following the incorporation of the City of Toledo, the Toledo-Lucas County Public Library has long served as this community's leader of information, education and inspiration.

From a single reading room on Summit Street to 19 locations throughout Lucas County, the "first free public library in Ohio" has long stood as a pillar of Northwest Ohio. Initially 66 individuals requested membership, looking to gain access to just under 500 books.

Usage and demand grew, and by 1873 the city of Toledo formed the Public Library of the City of Toledo. In 1890, the Main Toledo Public Library opened on Cherry Street with Frances Jermain as the first Library Director, and served the community through 1940.

In 1916 renowned library philanthropist Andrew Carnegie gave the City of Toledo $125,000 for the construction of branch libraries throughout Toledo. From these monies, the Locke, Kent, Mott, Jermain and South Branch Libraries were constructed, and many of them served the public into the next century.

The early part of the 20th century saw the Toledo Library introduce bookmobile service, specialized departments focusing on Children, Technology and Local History and opened several additional branches, including Birmingham, Lagrange, Point Place, Toledo Heights, Washington and West Toledo.

By the mid 1930s, Main Library had outgrown its current home and began looking for a new location. In 1938, the 100th anniversary of the formation of Toledo's first library, ground was broken on a new Main Library. On September 4, 1940, Main Library opened on Michigan Avenue. It stands at this location today, serving as a downtown landmark for generations.

Renowned worldwide for its classic art deco features, the large display of glass Vitrolite and a seamless blend of education and technology, Main Library remains to this day one of the cornerstones of Toledo, and a true jewel of Lucas County.

325 Michigan Street • Toledo, OH
419•259•5207 • toledolibrary.org

Toledo-Lucas County Public LIBRARY

:: The Toledo Hospital

Honoring the Past ... Celebrating the Future

The Renaissance Project –
scheduled to be completed in 2007

When The City Hospital of Toledo was established in 1874, Toledo was only 37 years old and had a population of 40,000. Over the next 130 years, The Toledo Hospital's services grew with the needs of the region. Today, The Toledo Hospital is the largest acute-care facility in the area, serving 23 counties in northwest Ohio and southeast Michigan. To continue our rich tradition of service, The Toledo Hospital is embarking upon the *Renaissance Project*, which will rebuild and expand facilities, enhance the delivery of services and exceed tomorrow's standards – *today*. Our commitment to caring continues a time-honored tradition that spans generations.

Member of

PROMEDICA
HEALTH SYSTEM

HOME SWEET HOME.

Toledo contractor, John Zakrzewski, built this home for his family in 1892. Standing behind the wooden sidewalk at 153 Dexter Street are his wife Maryanna and their children. Seven-month-old Edward is being held by his mother, as Casimer, Stella, and Julia peer at the camera. John added a second story to the home, which is still in use, in 1902. *Submitted by Larry and Mary Alice Kish. Mary Alice is a grand-daughter of Maryanna Zakrzewski.*

CEMETERY COMING HERE.

Two men stand atop a newly constructed dam on the Ottawa River in what was Washington Township in 1878. Behind them is a lake the dam had created to be a part of Toledo's first rural cemetery. The founding of Woodlawn Cemetery had occurred two years before, and its site encompassed 160 acres on Central Avenue, about three miles from Toledo's downtown. The rural cemetery movement was flourishing across the country and Toledo became a part of it with the establishment of Woodlawn. Designers emphasized a natural look and stressed original-ity in monument and mausoleum design. The result is a cemetery that doubles as a magnifi-cent park, bird sanctuary, and arboretum. Woodlawn was chosen by many of Toledo's early community and business leaders as their final resting place. *Submitted by the Woodlawn Cemetery Association.*

A SIGHTFUL BUSINESS.

Louis Beckmann, a German immigrant formally educated and trained in Europe, established his retail optical and survey instrument manufacturing businesses in Toledo in 1874. His first location was on St. Clair Street and was described in the Toledo City Directory for 1874-1875 as "manufacturer, surveying, mathematical instruments, and electric annunciators." Later, the retail business was operated at this location at 319 Adams Street, while the manufacturing branch was located on Jackson Street. Beckmann died in 1914 and the business was continued by his son, Louis, Jr. The enterprise continued over the years, and, in 1958, was one of only an estimated ten firms in the country specializing in the manufacture and repair of surveying instruments and components in America. Today the Beckmann name is displayed at the successor company, City BluePrint of Toledo, Inc. *Submitted by Tom Parker.*

TOLEDO BRANDS.

The Toledo Carriage Wood Work Company began operations in 1870 as manufacturers of shafts, poles, bows, hubs, spokes, rims, etc. from wood. The company incorporated in 1880 and transacted trade of their "Toledo Brands" line of products all over the United States. It's facility was a three-story brick building located on the Maumee River, between Lagrange and Cedar streets. *Submitted by Tom Parker.*

A DAPPER PAIR.

Otto August Dieball and his son, Earnest Edward Dieball, pose for a studio photographer circa 1881. Mr. Dieball, his wife, Sarah, and their family, lived on Marion Street in South Toledo. He worked as a machinist. *Submitted by Dean C. Dieball, grandson of Otto and son of Earnest.*

BAKERY DELIVERY.

Frank Kruse sits atop an M. Seyfang and Co. wagon in front of his home at 426 Havre Street in South Toledo. His wife, Caroline, and son, Walter, look on from the porch. M. Seyfang and Co. was a wholesale baker that initially operated at 11-19 Superior Street (Market Square) and later in the 800 block of Lafayette Street. Matthew and Frederick Seyfang, both of German birth, formed the wholesale baking company in 1888 from the Seyfang & Scherman bakery business that began operations in Toledo in 1864. In 1897, the company produced 10,000 loaves of bread and 100 barrels of crackers each day for distribution in Ohio, Michigan and Indiana. The business continued until circa 1915. *Submitted by Eleanor Gaisser, granddaughter of Frank Kruse.*

READY TO RIDE.

Charles James Dusseau, Jr. (4), and his brother, Melvin (2), are strapped in and ready for a ride in 1897. Their parents, Charles and Beatrice Dusseau, lived on Parkwood Avenue. Charles, Sr. was later the proprietor of Charles J. Dusseau & Sons, retailers of bicycles, children's vehicles, and baby and doll carriages at 2032-2034 Adams Street. *Submitted by Joann Dusseau Swanger, son of Charles James Dusseau, Jr.*

MYSTERY HOUSE.

Although not positively identified, evidence suggests that this is the Olds family home at 1114 Utah Street in East Toledo. If that is the case, the structure dates from 1867. This photograph is circa 1890 and features the family, formally dressed, along with what appears to be the household staff. The Olds family operated a nearby grocery store at 121 Fassett Street. *Submitted by Dan Crots.*

7

A TOLEDO JEWEL.

George U. Roulet, a Swiss immigrant, founded what is now The Roulet Company, manufacturing jewelers, in Toledo in 1877. Mr. Roulet appears to the right and next to the lady. This photograph is believed to have been taken at the company's Summit Street store in the late 19th century. Though the company has had numerous names, various partners, and several downtown locations through the years, its Roulet family ownership has been a constant and it is one of Toledo's oldest continuously operating businesses. *Submitted by The Roulet Company.*

FAMILY FARM.

The Bibb family home and dairy farm on Sterns Road in Bedford Township, Michigan, is shown here circa 1897. The three people just inside the gate are the owners Orin and Alice Pickard Bibb and their daughter, Myrtle. The other men are hired farm hands. The farm had been established by Orin's grandfather, Richard Bibb, a native of Wales, who arrived at the site in 1833. Milk produced on the farm was sold to Toledo dairies or made into butter which Orin sold on a route. The farm house was made from oak and walnut from the farm and built on an 18 inch thick limestone foundation circa 1850. Ownership of the house remained with the family until the 1980s, and it still stands at 1848 Sterns Road. *Submitted by Roland Strauss, grandson of Orin Bibb.*

MEAT MARKET.

Frank David, on the far right, stands in front of the meat market that bears his name. Joseph Birke stands to his right in this 1890 photograph. This store was located at 734 Bush Street. In 1891, Mr. David moved across the street to 806 Bush, but remained at the intersection of Ontario Street. The interior photograph was taken in 1894 with Frank David at the butcher block. *Submitted by Constance Hoffman, granddaughter of Frank David.*

FARM FAMILIES GATHER.

Several families gathered for this photograph circa 1900 at a farmhouse, perhaps on Wynn Road, in eastern Lucas County in what is now Oregon, Ohio. The adults are identified. Sitting from the left are Nancy Wynn, Samuel Jacobs, Thomas Wynn (holding Gordon Gilmore), Aunt Kate, Norma Douglas, and Charles Douglas. Standing from the left are: Margaret Cummings, Mr. Cummings, Clarisia Wynn Jacobs, Clara Jacobs, Norma Grummond, Nancy Helen Jacobs, Elsie Gilmore, David Gilmore, and Mable Curtis. It is thought that Wynn and Jacobs roads are named for families represented here. *Submitted by Nancy Wynn Hinds, granddaughter of Elsie and David Gilmore, great-granddaughter of Samuel Jacobs, and great-great-granddaughter of Nancy Wynn and Clarisia Wynn Jacobs.*

9

CIVIC PIONEER.

The Blade, on reporting Noah H. Swayne's death in 1922, said, "Probably no man in the last 50 years was more closely identified with the social, political, religious, and financial life of the city than Mr. Swayne." Swayne, the son of a U.S. Supreme Court Justice, came to Toledo in 1870. Over the years, he formed law partnerships with his brother Frank, Birchard Hayes (son of the sitting President), Julian Tyler (later a judge), and Rathbun Fuller. He was a bank director, a director and president for eight years of The Toledo Public Library board and served on many civic commissions, one of which, brought Edward Drummond Libbey to Toledo. He served in the Ohio legislature where he was the primary force in establishing the Toledo State Hospital. Swayne promoted radical changes to Toledo's water system, served on the committee to build the Lucas County Courthouse and provided funds to purchase the Smead School, precursor to the Maumee Valley Country Day School. Swayne's most known legacy is Swayne Field, Toledo's landmark baseball park. He was a director of Toledo's first professional club in 1883 and maintained his baseball interests all his life. *Submitted by John R. Husman.*

10

HIGH SIGN.

Albert Charles Walter founded his undertaking and embalming business in 1894. His first building, shown here, was at 1221 Broadway and featured a sign prominently placed atop the roof. Most likely, it is the proprietor himself, facing the camera in this circa 1900 photograph. *Submitted by the Walter Funeral Home.*

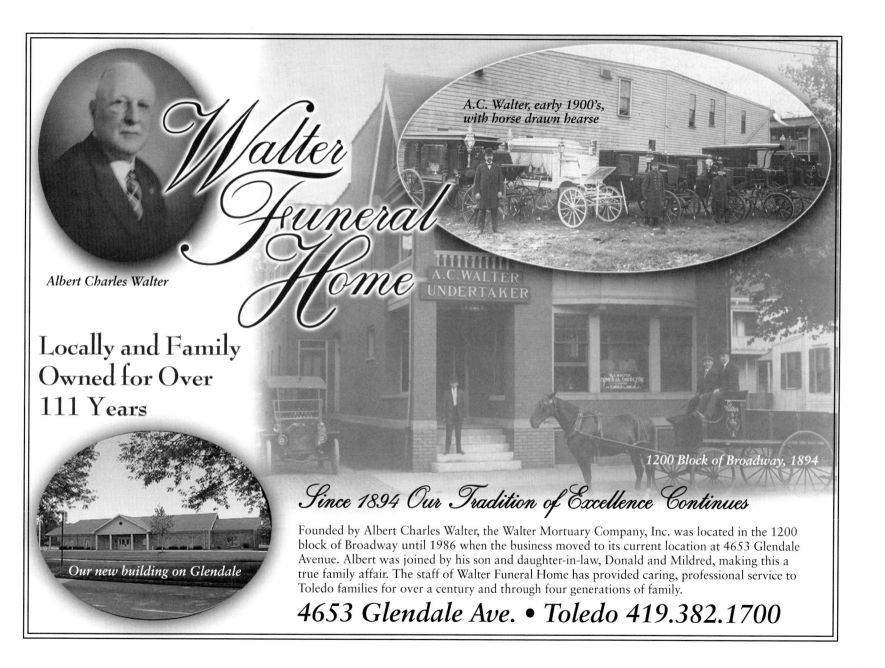

Albert Charles Walter

Walter Funeral Home

A.C. Walter, early 1900's, with horse drawn hearse

A.C. WALTER UNDERTAKER

Locally and Family Owned for Over 111 Years

Our new building on Glendale

1200 Block of Broadway, 1894

Since 1894 Our Tradition of Excellence Continues

Founded by Albert Charles Walter, the Walter Mortuary Company, Inc. was located in the 1200 block of Broadway until 1986 when the business moved to its current location at 4653 Glendale Avenue. Albert was joined by his son and daughter-in-law, Donald and Mildred, making this a true family affair. The staff of Walter Funeral Home has provided caring, professional service to Toledo families for over a century and through four generations of family.

4653 Glendale Ave. • Toledo 419.382.1700

playground was also equipped with swings, see-saws, slides, sand piles and a May pole. Behind the Armory is the spire of St. Mary's Catholic Church on Cherry Street.

At the dedication, Mayor Jones said that the playground, costing less than $1,000 to equip and run, was of greater value to the City than the county jail that had recently been constructed a block away, at Spielbusch and Jackson. He predicted that in years to come, the playground property would be "holy ground," a place where children could play, "safe from the temptations of the street." Unfortunately, the playground lasted only one summer and, ironically, the "holy ground" is now the site of the Lucas County Juvenile Justice Center. *Submitted by and caption written by Rolf Scheidel.*

TOLEDO'S FIRST PUBLIC PLAYGROUND.

Toledo's first public playground opened on July 26, 1899, and was situated in Toledo's poorest neighborhood on a two-acre parcel of the abandoned Miami and Erie Canal. Over 500 children attended the dedication ceremony conducted by Mayor Samuel "Golden Rule" Jones. According to The Blade, "Children young and old, white, black and tan, in silks and rags, and a majority barefoot, enjoyed a gala day on the new playground."

The playground was located on Spielbusch Avenue at Smith Street, across from the Lucas County Armory as shown. The top photograph shows boys enjoying the swinging rings. The

CLEANING CREW.

At least three carpet cleaning firms bearing the Kieswetter name have operated in Toledo. The first, The Kieswetter Carpet Cleaning and Rug Manufacturing Company, was established in 1882. Shown here are the J. F. Kieswetter Company offices at 828 Michigan Street. This company began circa 1903. The Joseph F. Kieswetter family also lived at this address. The company wagon, with employees on and about it, is adorned with an advertisement that reads, "Ohio Suction Carpet Cleaner." *Submitted by Mea Vendt.*

WOLCOTT HOUSE.

Family members relax on the front porch of the Wolcott House, on River Road in Maumee, Ohio, circa 1905. The young woman poised to ride off on her bicycle is thought to be the great-granddaughter of James Wolcott, who built the Federal style home overlooking the Maumee River in the early 1830s. Wolcott, a native of Connecticut and descendant of Oliver Wolcott, signer of the Declaration of Independence, was a successful entrepreneur who served as a Lucas County Common Pleas Judge, mayor of Maumee, organizer of the Lucas County Whig Party, and a wholesaler, and ship builder. His docks and warehouses were situated in front of the mansion. Wolcott's wife, Mary, was the daughter of William Wells, noted Indian scout and agent, and Sweet Breeze, a daughter of the Miami Chief, Little Turtle. The house remained in the Wolcott family until 1957 when it became a museum and home of the Maumee Valley Historical Society. *Submitted by the Maumee Valley Historical Society. Caption written by Marilyn Wendler.*

PEACEFUL SCENE.

Henrietta Suder sits in the dining room of her home at 2941 Cherry Street on December 27, 1894. Her husband, Ewald, had been the superintendent of Lenk & Company's (wine makers) greenhouse prior to establishing his own floral gardens and greenhouse on Cherry Street. Ewald died at age 39 in 1881, and Henrietta continued the operation. Today, the Suder family credits Henrietta with being Toledo's first florist, beginning in 1870. The business continued as a family operation until its doors closed in 1988. Henrietta is also remembered by the street named for her – Suder Avenue. *Submitted by William A. Suder, great-grandson of Henrietta Suder.*

A GREAT REFLECTION!

John P. Sattler manufactured and sold cigars at this store at 707 South St. Clair Street. He and his wife, Eilzabeth Adams Sattler, made their home here as well. Shown with him in this circa 1896 image are three of the five children born to the couple. The taller girl is Mary, her sister is Tresa and her brother is Carl. Tresa later married George Pierce and became the mother of this photograph's donor. The buildings from across the street are clearly reflected in Sattler's windows. The awnings on those buildings have the names of businesses on them that are partially seen in reverse image. The Toledo City Directory for 1896 confirms that Gessner & Beckman grocery and J.G. Vollmayer Meats and Sausage Factory are those businesses. Farther down the opposite side of the street, and in the same block, was (and is) Saints Peter and Paul Catholic Church and just a block away on South Erie Street was (and is) St. John's Lutheran Church. These churches and shops were the heart of a near south side German neighborhood. *Submitted by Patricia P. Munger, daughter of Tresa Sattler Pierce.*

14

CHRISTMAS MEATS.

The West End Meat Market occupies the right side of this brick building at 1203 Dorr Street. George Fleischman, Sr., hand on hip, the proprietor, stands at the corner of the building. The left side of the building (1201 Dorr Street at Hoag Street) houses Will Cangrey's barber shop, and displays an advertisement for the Buckeye Steam Laundry. Both Fleischman and Cangrey made their homes above their businesses. The interior view of The West End Market shows the store, decorated for Christmas, with George and his children, George, Jr. and Elorna. Both photographs are from 1890. Notice the hitching posts, trolley rails, plank road and plank sidewalk. George, Sr. later built and owned the Atlas, World, and State theaters. *Submitted by Mary Ann Thurber, granddaughter of George Fleischman, Sr.*

SMOKEY STEAMER.

The side-wheel steamer METROPOLIS departs from downtown Toledo sometime between 1894 and 1902 and heads downriver. She was built in Trenton, Michigan in 1868 and operated on Lakes Huron and Superior before being sold to Toledo interests in 1894. Upper works and cabins, suitable for the excursion business were added and she ran from Toledo to Put-In-Bay and Monroe. The METROPOLIS burned on June 13, 1902. Several buildings/businesses can be identified in this smokey scene: Stolberg & Parks, manufactures and dealers in furniture, The Boody House Hotel, and the Niagara Hotel, offering 15-cent meals. *Submitted by Bill and Shirley Douge.*

ON THE BOARDWALK.

Kathryn Rickens Schmitt, wife of John Schmitt, stands on a wooden walkway outside her Nebraska Avenue home with her daughter, Kathryn, one and a half years old, and infant son, Leo, circa 1899. *Submitted by Rita Roth Cark.*

A LUCKEY SALOON.

Tony Kroetz operated this establishment that offered refreshments at the corner of Main and Walnut streets in Luckey from 1893 until 1913. This photograph is from about 1900. It was, in fact, a saloon offering Toledo's Buckeye Beer as shown by the advertisements on the building's corners. Kroetz indicated that he earned his living as a brewery agent to the 1910 Federal census enumerator. A free lunch of hard boiled eggs, cold cuts, cheese and bread were put out for the customers to enjoy with their beer. To the proprietor's dismay, however, some came in for the free lunch and never bought a drink. Tony Kroetz catered to the ladies as well. A lady of the time would ruin her reputation if she was seen in a saloon, so the enterprising saloon keeper provided a solution. A side entrance on Walnut Street allowed a lady to enter the bar and have her drink in a private room and not be observed. *Submitted by Tom Parker.*

PATRIOTIC GATHERING.

Joseph Bernard Thomas, top row, middle, with arms crossed, was about 13 years old and an apprentice tool and die maker when this picture was taken circa 1891. Perhaps this was an Independence Day or other patriotic occasion, as this gathering of workers, at The Vulcan Iron Works of Toledo, is framed with American flag-like bunting. *Submitted by Judy Lebowsky Shook, granddaughter of Joseph Bernard Thomas.*

POLE CLIMBERS.

Little is known about this early photograph of an electric utility line crew. It appears to be in the Toledo area from the sign, seen just over the horse's back, which advertises property for sale. The sign was placed by "Robert J. Law Real Estate, 236 Huron Street." The latest entry for Mr. Law in the Toledo city directories at this address is 1902. It seems reasonable that this fine photograph was taken in or near Toledo circa 1900. Note the similarity of the climbing equipment to that in use today. *Submitted by Sharon Yaros.*

17

A BIG HOUSE.

Dr. J. Lee Richmond sits on the steps of his home at 718 West Grove Place circa 1901. His wife, Mary, sits on the porch and the first of his three daughters, Ruth, poses with her bicycle. Dr. Richmond came to Toledo in 1890 and was an educator here for nearly 40 years. He taught at Toledo and Scott high schools, was principal at East Side High School, and, later, Professor and Dean of Men at Toledo University. A former professional baseball player, Richmond had pitched major league's first perfect game in 1880. The Richmond home was later moved west to 746 West Grove Place to make room for the Toledo Museum of Art. *Submitted by Marianne H. Quellhorst, great-great-granddaughter of J. Lee Richmond.*

THE TRILBY STORE.

The Trilby Store was built in 1901 by Giles Pelton at the northwest corner of Alexis Road and Pearl (now Gay) Street. The store and the platting of his 40 acre farm as Trilby Place, coincided with the coming of the Toledo and Western Railroad, an electric-powered interurban line that paralleled Tremainsville and Alexis roads. He also built the livery stable behind the store. Here, customers from the Trilby area and nearby Bedford and Whiteford townships could board their horses while taking the interurban streetcars into the city. The small white shed between the store and stable contained a supply of flammable kerosene to sell for lighting homes and barns in the rural area. Orra Pelton assisted his father and later managed the business.

In 1918, brothers Lee and Smith Janney took over the operation. In 1927, Smith Janney moved the hardware business to the southwest corner of Alexis and Secor roads where it continues today in the third generation. Lee continued the grocery business at the former general store. *Submitted by Ken Levin. Caption written by Fred J. Folger, great-grandson of Giles Pelton.*

18

BUSY INTERSECTION-TO-BE.

This amazing photograph shows the crossing of two dirt, country roads. Alexis extends across the picture and Secor extends from the lower left to the upper right. Orra Pelton climbed a farmyard windmill in 1902 and pointed his camera northwest to capture the gathering of local residents who stand in the center of the intersection to view the flooding waters of Silver Creek. The Toledo and Western RR track parallels Alexis Road. When completed, the electric interurban line provided freight and passenger service between Toledo and Pioneer with a branch to Adrian, Michigan. The headquarters were in Sylvania. The T&W ceased operation in 1932. Today, Alexis and Secor roads number among the busiest and most congested thoroughfares in Toledo. *Submitted by and caption written by Fred Folger.*

BUFFALO HOUSE.

Edward Zumbrunn, Sr. stands to the far right at his home at 726 Buffalo Street circa 1900. His wife Marie is standing on the porch, wearing dark clothing. Seated near her, and similarly dressed, is her mother, Barbara Shearer. To Edward's right, is his son Edward, Jr. Another son, Walter sits on the railing, directly above his brother, John, who is with his son, Norman, and wife, Minnie, sitting to the left on the steps. The other lady sitting on the steps is Edward's daughter, Emilie. Directly behind her and near the post is Lena Liske, thought to be a cousin visiting from Switzerland. *Submitted by Barbara Carr, great-great-granddaughter of Barbara Shearer, great-granddaughter of Marie Zumbrunn, and granddaughter of Emilie Zumbrunn.*

19

NEIGHBORHOOD GROCERY.

Neighborhood groceries abounded as the 20th century began. Many people shopped daily, and close to where they lived, as they did not have the means to store food safely at home. Here, Giovanni (John) Mercurio stands in front of his store, at 1313 Washington Street in 1902. On display are some fresh produce items for his neighborhood. Mr. Giovanni died in 1904. *Submitted by Giroma Nera, granddaughter of Giovanni (John) Mercurio.*

FISH MARKET.

George M. Goulden, second from the left, moved the business established by his father (see page 2) to 617 Monroe Street in 1902. The Monroe street business focused on fish and poultry, with an apparent emphasis on fish. Goulden dubs his store as the "Oyster Depot," and has a young man holding a huge "fish" attention-getter. His three wagons, shown here, are heavy with advertising, including the motto, "Not How Cheap But How Good." Goulden's building was destroyed by fire in 1998, though the west wall remains. The fire ruined this block's claim as the only complete block (south side of Monroe Street between Huron and Erie streets) of century-old buildings left in Toledo. *Submitted by Mary Pat Carter Reifsnider, granddaughter of George Goulden.*

20

A BAND OF NEWSBOYS.

The Newsboys Association Band poses in front of the offices of their newspapers, The Toledo Times and The News-Bee circa 1908. The Newsboys Association was founded on Christmas Day, 1892 by John Gunckel. The association promoted self-worth for young men. Gunkle's organization fostered the Boys and Girls Clubs of today and many of its alumni were founders of, and active participants in The Old Newsboys Goodfellows Association. It has been said of Gunckel, "He didn't make money, he made men." *Submitted by The Old Newsboys Goodfellows Association, Richard H. Buchholz, Historian.*

CIRCUS PARADE.

The Adam Forepaugh and Sells Brothers Big United Shows circus parade is proceeding east on Monroe Street on August 4, 1901. Escorted by bicyclists, the lead horses are just entering the Huron Street intersection. The trolley tracks and bricks are long gone from Monroe Street, but many of these buildings remain. *Submitted by John Connors.*

TWO GENTS, THREE HATS.

Frederick Anthony Fleischman takes notes or keeps score at a baseball game while holding up a pair of hats. Father Redding, wearing only one hat, looks on at the game at St. Mary's Catholic Church (German) in 1904. Notice the baseball bat at their feet. *Submitted by Mary Angela Keller.*

A TO Z MARKET.

Andrew Zeiler arrived in Toledo in 1888 and established this grocery at 1202 Moore Street, at the corner of Chestnut. This 1904 photograph reveals, by the sign on the awning, that Zeiler also operated a saloon that had an entrance on the Chestnut Street side. All here are identified, including Molly, the horse. From the left, the people are: Joseph, Andrew, Sr., Leo, Andrew, Jr. (behind the stroller), Matilda (next to stroller), Theresa (in stroller), Edward, Grandmother Theresa, Gretchen (at the saloon entrance), and a neighbor, Gertrude. In all, the Zeilers had 11 children. Andrew sold the store in 1908 and became a farmer on Angola Road. *Submitted by David Roberts, grandson of Andrew Zeiler, Sr. and son of Theresa Zeiler.*

PEDDLIN' PAPERS.

William J. Harbright stands tall as a newspaper delivery boy for the Toledo Blade circa 1907. Bill was born in Toledo, January 15, 1896 and served in the United States Army during World War I. *Submitted by Betty Lloyd, grand-niece of William Harbright.*

EAST LOOKING WEST.

The Cherry Street bridge stretches across the Maumee River from The Toledo & Ohio Central Railroad yards in the foreground in this 1904 photograph. The building is the railroad's Main Street Depot. The bridge is congested with street-car and horse and buggy traffic. Water street industry dominates the west river bank. *Submitted by and caption written by Ron Mauter.*

ELECTRIC SPIN.

Sisters, Mrs. Erwin Robert Effler (nee Fanny Pilliod) and Mrs. John F. Kumler, (nee Teresa Pilliod), enjoy a ride in a Baker electric automobile circa 1906. Baker manufactured such vehicles between 1899 and 1915, and this was one of the first to be seen on Toledo's streets. Electric automobiles could travel up to 20 miles per hour and had a range of 20 to 50 miles on a charging of the batteries. Women reportedly favored electrics because they did not require cranking and had no exhaust fumes. *Submitted by Fanny Effler, granddaughter of Mrs. Erwin Robert Effler.*

SILVER JUBILEE.

The silver jubilee of Reverend G. H. Rieken is celebrated at Saints Peter and Paul Catholic Church, on South St. Clair Street on July 4, 1905. Father Rieken was Pastor of the parish 1904-1912. The church was established in 1866 by German-American families and has also served the Hispanic community since 1927. *Submitted by Father Richard E. Notter, Pastor, Saints Peter and Paul Church.*

SADDLE UP.

John G. Widmaier stands to the right in this circa 1905 photograph of the interior of his harness shop at 114 North St. Clair Street. His sons, Carl (on the left) and Joe, work at the benches while keeping an eye on the camera. Mr. Widmaier's stationery advertised that his business was "manufacturer of harness of every description and dealer in saddles, blankets, whips, combs, brushes, nets, boots, and all kinds of horse clothing." He also stated, "fine harness to order a specialty." It appears that the shop had a variety of tools to do custom work. This building housed a harness business from the 1870s until the early 1930s. *Submitted by James Blum, grandnephew of John G. Widmaier.*

SERIOUS BUSINESS.

Some New York Central Railroad office staff members strike a serious pose on May 3, 1906. This storekeeper's office was located at the Airline Junction yards near Fearing Street and Detroit Avenue. Airline Junction was an expansive railroad yard located near the south side of Hill Avenue. It extended from east of Detroit Avenue to west of Byrne Road. It was developed in the 1870s to accommodate various railroads which served Toledo. The name derived from the Air Line RR, completed in 1857, from Chicago, across northern Indiana and northwest Ohio, to Toledo. It featured a 68 1/2-mile stretch of straight track between the junction and Butler, Indiana. An early neighborhood for railroad workers developed by the rail yard and had its own post office with an Airline Junction postmark. Standing at the far left is Mae Quilter while her brother, Edward Quilter, stands just to the right of and behind the table. Fred Taylor, standing far right, later married Mae. Mae was an aunt of Barney Quilter, long-time member of the Ohio General Assembly. *Submitted by the Taylor family.*

BIG SCOOP.

William Allen Westfall puts this huge steam shovel through its paces circa 1906. Mr. Westfall was a foreman for the Vulcan Steam Shovel Company of Toledo, manufacturer of this machine, and was involved in performance testing for the big rigs. *Submitted by Gary Westfall, grandson of William Westfall.*

THE ORIGINAL COYLE.

This photograph shows the original building of the Coyle Funeral Home circa 1903. James Coyle founded this business at Broadway and Logan streets in 1888. James Coyle is standing to the right, along with his son, William Coyle and Winefred. *Submitted by Dan Bosch.*

GERMAN GROCERIES AND CIGARS.

Herman C. Teschner operated this store and made his residence at 810 Galena Street (near Ontario Street) in 1906. He advertised groceries, cigars and tobacco, but plenty of fresh fruit is on display, as well. The worker on the left is Henry Oswald Drager who was about 19 years old at the time this picture was taken. He lived his life in Toledo, working as a self-employed carpenter and died in 1953 at age 66. *Submitted by Howard Drager, son of Henry Oswald Drager.*

THE EYES HAVE IT.

Howard Newton Warner stands before his jewelry and optometry store at 2118 Lawrence Avenue in 1903. Warner was a graduate of the Detroit School of Optometry and the eye on his window indicates that he offered those services. In addition, one could purchase jewelry, watches, clocks, cigars, and tobacco. The sign on the awning indicates that this was also "The Lawrence Avenue News Depot." Warner's dog was named Major. *Submitted by Nancy Stonerock, granddaughter of Howard N. Warner.*

DOG ON RUNNING BOARD.

Charles H. Schroeder proudly sits behind the wheel of a new automobile he won in a drawing circa 1916. His wife, Beatrice, and daughter, Edna, are the passengers, while his huge dog covers the running board. The photograph was probably taken at Mr. Schroeder's Forsythe Street home in East Toledo. *Submitted by Dick Schroeder, grandson of Charles H. Schroeder.*

27

PLAY BALL!

Amateur baseball flourished in Toledo, as elsewhere in the country early in the twentieth century. This team photograph from 1904 depicts the team representing The Toledo Railways and Light Company. On the left in the front row is Billy Ragan. The other reclining player is unidentified. Seated, from the left, are, Jim Robison, Patrick J. Boyle and Tony Bialecki. In the back row, from the left, are Houtz, Larkin, Hathaway, P. Gus Rieder, Henry Prenberger, and Bill Ashe. Boyle, an Irish immigrant born in County Tyrone, was the team's Captain and a Division Superintendent for The Community Traction Company. Among his five children was Mary Boyle Burns, who was active for many years in Lucas County and Ohio Democratic Party affairs. *Submitted by Mary Kay Solt, great-granddaughter of Patrick J. Boyle.*

FUNERAL IN WHITE.

This photograph of a funeral, probably that of a child, was held at St. Stephen's Catholic Church (Hungarian) on Consaul Street in East Toledo. This building, the first of three for the congregation, served from 1899 to 1908, when it was destroyed by fire. Yolanda Szuch explained the white attire when discussing funerals in her History of St. Stephen's Church. "They [Hungarians] see it as a wedding, since their neighbor has become the bridegroom of Heaven. In fact, in most parts of Hungary at the turn of the century, the people would hold a ceremonial wedding on the death of a young boy or girl. In Toledo, some parishioners remember young girls dressed in white, as if a bride, when buried." *Submitted by Betty Holub, lifetime member of St. Stephen's Church.*

THE UNIVERSITY OF TOLEDO

A University of Distinction since 1872

FLORAL WAGON.

Walter ImOberstag stands with his foot on the wheel of his floral delivery wagon in front of his Western Avenue greenhouse in May, 1906. His business address was 1531 Western Avenue and his horse was named Banker. Walter's sister was Myrtle, the namesake of today's Myrtle Flowers. *Submitted by Doris Ott, niece of Walter and daughter of Myrtle ImOberstag.*

HOTEL WINDMILL.

Hotel guests and people in Curtice, Ohio, gather under the windmill outside the Hotel Dunn for this circa 1907 photograph. Charles Frank Dunn had entered the hotel business in Curtice in 1895, and opened this building on July 4, 1907. Mr. Dunn later added a livery business and in 1911, a garage. By then he had obtained the agency of the Buick, King, Hudson, and Dart automobiles in Curtice. The former Hotel Dunn building still stands at 1750 North Lucas Street, at Front Street in Curtice. *Submitted by James C. Dunn, grandson of Charles Frank Dunn.*

CHEERS!

Every man in the Frank Iwinski and Son Saloon is raising a glass of dark beer. Though Christmas decorations remain above the bar, calendars on the wall reveal that this photograph was taken in March, 1907. Iwinski's saloon was located at 745 Detroit Avenue. *Submitted by Daniel F. Drzewiecki.*

SIX GENERATIONS.

Four generations of women pose in 1907 for the photograph on the left. Lucille Hoffmann is the young lady in the center. Moving clockwise are: her great-grandmother, Theresa Miller: her mother, Ida Welling Hoffmann; and her grandmother; Sophia Miller Welling. The photograph, at the top of the page, was taken in 1915 and depicts five generations. Lucille is now Lucille Hoffmann Garbe at the upper right. Clockwise from her are: Theresa Miller holding baby Louise Garbe (Lucille's daughter), Ida Welling Hoffmann, and Sophia Miller Welling. The final photograph is of five generations and is dated 1935. Lucille is at the upper right. Clockwise from her are: Sophia Miller Welling, Louise Garbe Bruggeman holding baby, Marcia Bruggeman (her daughter), and Ida Welling Hoffmann. The beauty of these photographs can only be described as breathtaking. *Submitted by William Garbe, son of Lucille Hoffman Garbe, etc.*

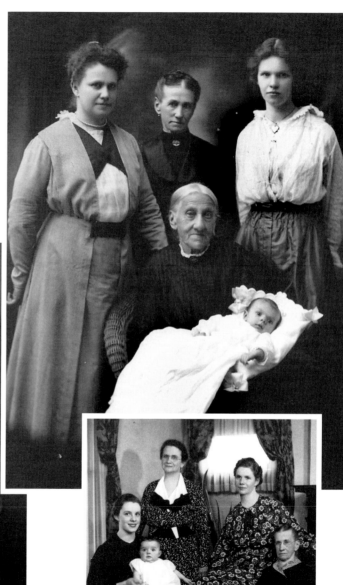

31

MUD HEN AND MASTER MANAGER.

Joe McCarthy is shown here in action at Swayne Field in Toledo in 1910. McCarthy was a utility player, batting .231 in 350 games in his four years as a Mud Hen, 1908-1911. He never made it to the major leagues as a player, but he did as a manager. And how! McCarthy managed 24 seasons in the major leagues and has the highest winning percentage of any manager, ever. He was the first manager to win a pennant in both major leagues and was the first pennant-winning manager without major league playing experience. In all, he won nine pennants, finished second seven times, and never finished in the second division, nor had a losing season while leading the Chicago Cubs, New York Yankees and Boston Red Sox. Swayne Field, located at Monroe Street and Detroit Avenue, was the home of professional baseball in Toledo from 1909 until 1955. This rare baseball photograph was found by Mark Walczak. *Submitted by The Toledo Mud Hens Baseball Club.*

THE INDIAN TREE   MAUMEE, OHIO

INDIAN ELM.

According to legend, a Native American sniper found refuge in this once magnificent tree while shooting American soldiers on the banks of the Maumee River below Fort Meigs during the War of 1812. Finally, an American sharpshooter was ordered to "drop him" to the ground. The sniper was silenced, but the legend lived on. The tree was so revered by later generations that Harrison Street was built around it. It stood, surviving lightning strikes, fire, and erratic drivers, until 1924, when it was removed to make way for the widening of Harrison Street. This photograph was taken shortly before the demise of the elm circa 1920. It looks east on Harrison Street and shows the homes of two early Maumee settlers, Morrison R. Waite, later Chief Justice of the United States, (center) and Mark Richardson (left). These historic homes continue to serve as residences and are on the National Register of Historic Places. A bronze plate, commissioned by residents, commemorates the site of the Indian Elm. *Submitted by Jack Hiles. Caption written by Marilyn Wendler.*

SWINGING WITH GRANDPA.

Jesse Nelson Dewey enjoys a sunny afternoon in September, 1914, on a swing in the backyard of his home at 2491 Glenwood Avenue, at Delaware Avenue. His is flanked by his grandchildren (clockwise); Jesse Dewey, Ruth Dewey Wolcott, Mary Lindsay, Dorothy Dewey, and Martha Leighton. *Submitted by Anthony Rodriguez (former owner of the Dewey house).*

CONFUSED HOUSE.

This house faces Hamilton Street, but its address is 316 Junction Avenue. The owners, Chester (near middle) and Angela (far right) Palicki, stand behind a wooden plank sidewalk circa 1908. Their daughter, Helen Wanda, is the child. Chester's brother, Frank Palicki, and his wife, Mary, are the other adults. *Submitted by Walter Palicki, grandnephew of Chester and Frank Palicki.*

BARRELS PILED HIGH.

Alton Delbert Barhite sits atop the beer kegs as he makes deliveries in downtown Toledo. This photograph was taken at 541 Erie Street circa 1910. *Submitted by Pat Anaszewicz, granddaughter of Alton Delbert Barhite.*

MILK BY MAUD.

Howard N. Warner pauses in front of this house at 130 Glenwood Road, in Rossford circa 1908. According to the sign on his wagon, he is delivering Warner's Jersey Milk to his customers. Pulling the wagon is Maud. *Submitted by Nancy Stonerock, granddaughter of Howard N. Warner.*

SHOE SALES STAFF.

The sales staff of the HM & R Shoe Company stands ready at their store at the corner of Summit and Adams streets. Frank Tucker is the gentleman with the moustache on the right in this circa 1911 photograph. Note the ceiling supports in this double-wide store. *Submitted by Dick Schroeder, grandson of Frank Tucker.*

IRONVILLE WICKETS.

Young people play croquet on the lawn of Ironville's Lincoln Place Park in 1910. The first building, on the left, is the Ironville Neighborhood House. The large buildings across Front Street are Hopkins Shoe Repair, on the left, and Mauter Brothers Blacksmith Shop. The park was located on Front Street near Millard Avenue, and later was the site of the Unitcast Steel Foundry. *Submitted by and caption written by Ron Mauter.*

FIRST IN TOLEDO SCOUTING.

The first Boy Scout troop in Toledo was organized October 1, 1910, at the YMCA on Michigan Avenue. The first Scoutmaster was William Hoffmeister who was the Boys' Work Secretary at the YMCA. Hoffmeister is the reclining gentleman in this photograph of Troop 1. Troop 2 was organized in December, 1910, at the Third Presbyterian Church with the Rev. John F. Sheppard serving as Scoutmaster. Troop 3 was organized by William Bolles in the spring of 1911 with the troop meeting at a log cabin Mr. Bolles built near his home. By 1912, there were ten Boy Scout troops in the city. *Submitted by Miakonda Scouting Museum, Erie Shores Council, Boy Scouts of America, David Eby, Historian. Caption written by David Eby.*

TWO VIEWS.

Two photographs, interior and exterior, of the J.G. Kuehnl Fancy Groceries and Meats store at 45 City Park Avenue are shown here. The structure was built circa 1908 and had a five-bedroom attached home which faced Green Street. There was also a barn and a stable on the property. Shown standing on the steps in 1911 are Joseph and Maria Kuehnl and their children Florence, Harold, and Caroline (being held by her mother). Previously Mr. Kuehnl had been a manufacturer and distributor of patent medicines. A desire for less travel prompted Mr. Kuehnl to enter the grocery business and an inheritance from Austria made it possible. The photograph of the interior of the store is circa 1929. Alice Kuehnl is in front of the meat counter. Behind the grocery counter are Caroline and Harold. The others are customers. *Submitted by Jean Carroll, daughter of Caroline Kuehnl.*

HOW TO SAVE GAS.

Gilbert Dahme, 15, stands in front of a Mathias Bippus & Son Grocers horse-drawn wagon in East Toledo in 1911. The grocery store was located at 322 Fassett Street. *Submitted by Linda Fravel, granddaughter of Gilbert Dahme.*

HOLD YOUR HORSES.

Clement "Clem" Wernert, son of Charles and Magdalena Wernert, is sitting in the J. P. Johnson Dairy, delivery carriage. Barney Thomas holds the horses in position on Moore Street at the corner of Walnut Street. Thomas was the proprietor of a grocery and saloon at that intersection. The saloon entrance can be seen behind the wagon's front wheels. Wernert used the carriage to make grocery deliveries for Thomas. John P. Johnson was in the dairy business from 1902 until 1924. *Submitted by Judy Lebowsky Shook, great-granddaughter of Bernard "Barney' Thomas.*

WHEN YOU WISH UPON A STAR.

Christmas wishes for brothers Gail, (left) and Don Hasse, came true in 1914. Under the tree at their 1911 Camden Street home were the tricycles the boys had hoped for. *Submitted by Judy Manders, daughter of Don Haase.*

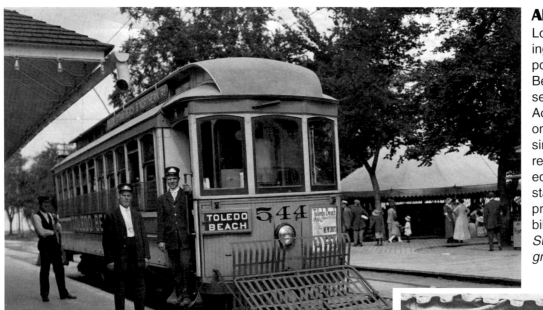

ALL ABOARD!

Louis Warren Cann is front and center and standing on the platform beside a Toledo Beach electric powered interurban car circa 1920. The Toledo Beach Line was formed in 1907 and provided service to the immensely popular resort area. According to Tana Mosier Porter, 15,000 people once rode cars such as this to Toledo Beach on a single day, Independence Day, 1907. She also reported that "By August, 1908, forty cars operated on the line, with a car leaving the interurban station every two minutes.... The interurbans prospered until trucks, buses and private automobiles began to replace them in the late 1920s." *Submitted by Robin and Alan Woody. Woody is a great-grandson of Louis Warren Cann.*

GROSS BEGINNING.

Jack Gross (left) poses with Gross Electric founder, George (Joe) Gross, circa 1910. The company was first known as The Toledo Gas Appliance Company and was located at 612 Jefferson Street. Initially, the Toledo company sold radios, mixers, toasters and other small appliances, as well as lighting fixtures like those shown here. *Submitted by Joe Gross, grandson of George (Joe) Gross.*

WOOD EVERYWHERE.

This photograph shows the home of the August and Bertha Goralska family at 1059 Buckingham Street circa 1910. Lumber was the material of choice for the fence and sidewalk, as well as the house itself. The lady holding the baby is Bertha Goralska and to her right is Marie Trost. *Submitted by Carlene Trost, granddaughter-in-law of Marie Trost.*

HATS AND GRASS.

These four ladies seem to enjoy showing off their fine hats at Willys Park in West Toledo circa 1910. From the left are sisters; Florence Feldman, Irene Feldman, and Agnes Feldman Melczak, and their cousin Irene Block. *Submitted by Marian R. Fisher, granddaughter of Agnes Feldman Melczak.*

39

CANAL BOAT HEADIN' THIS WAY!

This timber truss swing bridge once carried South Avenue traffic and pedestrians across the Miami & Erie Canal. Bridge tender, Scott Wible, stands poised to rotate a large version of a socket wrench to crank the bridge open and allow a boat to pass. A series of gears below allowed a single person to rotate the heavy span. The posted sign cautions "$5.00 FINE for being on the draw while in motion." This photo looks east across the canal. In the distance, the J. B. Pennyson Lumber Company, 1041 South Avenue, can be seen in this circa 1909 photograph. Toledo was the northern terminus of this canal (Wabash & Erie) which was completed from Indiana in 1843. Two years later a link joined this canal with the Miami Canal which served Cincinnati and Dayton. To avoid confusion, the all-Ohio route was officially named the Miami & Erie Canal in 1849. The peak year of operation was 1851. Railroads, with greater speed and year-round operation, quickly became the preferred means of transportation. Major flooding in 1913 brought the official closing of the canal for boat-use. After that year, a low, stationary bridge replaced the pictured draw bridge. The canal was drained in 1929 and filled, graded, and paved to become the Anthony Wayne Trail. *Submitted by Mark Walczak. Caption written by Fred Folger.*

HARDWARE HOME.

David Joseph Marleau stands with two boys in front of the first Toledo hardware store to bear his name. This store was at 414 Phillips Avenue in West Toledo and the photograph is circa 1910. A wide array of hardware and houseware items are on display and more can be seen through the windows on both floors. Justice of the Peace, Sheldon Stebbins, made his office on the second floor, left side. Mr. Marleau later moved his store to Dorr Street and then to Monroe Street. He retired circa 1940 and family members continued the business. *Submitted by Dorothy Schabeck, daughter of David Joseph Marleau.*

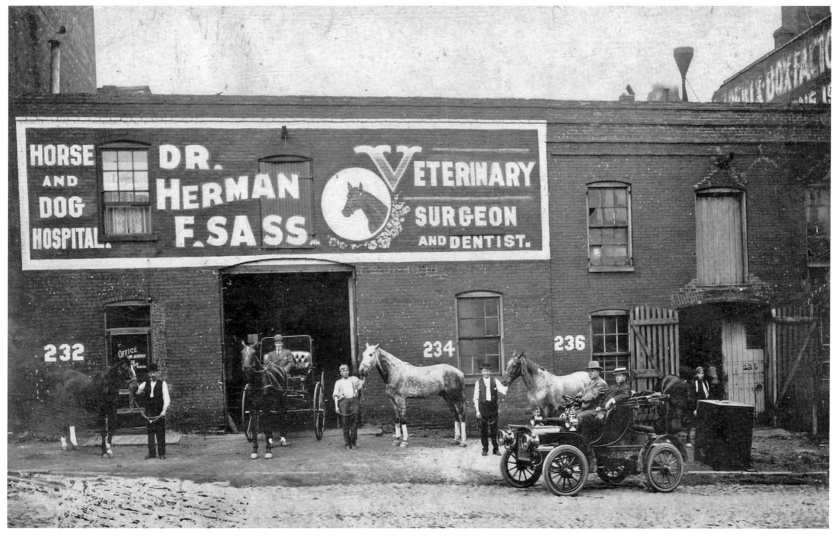

HORSE DOCTOR.

The veterinary hospital and boarding stable of long time Toledo grain merchant and veterinarian, Dr. Herman F. Sass, was located at 232-236 Vine Street, near the Cherry Street bridge. This photograph, circa 1911, shows various forms of transportation in use at that time. Dr. Sass retired in 1922, but the business was carried on for several years by his son Clarence. *Submitted by and caption written by Ken Levin.*

FATHER AND SON GROCERS.

Julius Petsch immigrated to America from Germany in 1882. He opened a grocery store at 801 Curtis Street in 1900, and then, after three years, moved his business to this store at 877 Curtis. He stands in the left doorway, wearing an apron. The doorway to the right is the entrance to a saloon he also operated. He continued there as he and his wife, Lena, reared a family of seven children. Three of his sons would follow him in the grocery business. Julius, Jr. and Carl continued at the Curtis Street location.

Bottom photo: Otto Petsch, son of Julius Petsch, Sr., worked as a bartender for several years, and then, he too, went into the grocery business. He opened, near his father, at 725 Segur Street in 1919. He stands in the door of his store with his wife, Hattie, and her mother, Mrs. Heins. Their daughter, Marcella, is standing on the sidewalk. As did his father, Otto also operated a saloon which is located next door in this photograph.

Both photographs submitted by Sandy Owen, great-granddaughter of Julius Petsch, Sr.

GROCERY AND SALOON.

Bernard "Barney" Thomas, born in Durrenbach, Alsace, France, operated this grocery and saloon at 2102 Walnut Street (corner Moore Street) from 1896 until 1912. He advertised, "Fine groceries and provisions, choice wines, liquors and cigars." Some of the people in the photograph are identified. Barney is seated in the chair and his wife, Magdalena "Lena" (nee Wernert) Thomas, stands directly behind him. Standing to their right are sisters (nee Knowles), Ada Fischer, and Ruth Brenneman. The Thomas family lived on the second floor. *Submitted by Judy Lebowsky Shook, great-granddaughter of Bernard "Barney' Thomas.*

MILK DELIVERY.

John Ernest Raitz pauses on his delivery route for this photograph circa 1911. Mr. Raitz delivered dairy products for George Grodi (Sr.) Farm Dairy. The young helper, peering out from inside the wagon is John Grodi, Jr. *Submitted by Constance Hoffman, daughter of John Raitz.*

MISNOMER.

These people, gathered under the arch circa 1910, are not "kids" as they advertise. They do have something to do with candy, however. The scene is the home of the Smith-Kirk Candy Company at 44-48 South Superior Street. Smith-Kirk was a manufacturer and whole saler of confectionary items. Agnes Braker was a chocolate dipper for the Toledo company which was headed by Jerome H. Smith. This building presently is the home of the Spaghetti Warehouse. *Submitted by Dorothy Pakulski, niece of Agnes Braker.*

HANGING BROOMS AND MORE.

The Raczkowski family operated a grocery store at the corner of Everett and Lagrange streets for 16 years. Husband Kaiser headed the business and housed his family at 2831 Lagrange Street beginning in 1904. After his death at age 34 due to a long illness of dropsy (edema) in 1914, his wife, Rose, continued the business. She moved next door to 2829 Lagrange (within the same building that still exists) and continued there until 1919. Although not identified, it may be Rose Raczkowski and one of her daughters, Margaret or Elsie shown here. Submitted by *Art Merrill.*

YOUNG FARMERS.

Peter and Hazel (nee Arquette) Jacobs are shown here circa 1912, when both were about 19 years old. By 1920, the couple was operating a farm on Cedar Point Road, Oregon Township, in eastern Lucas County, and had started a family. They had two daughters at the time, but were destined to have a family of eight children – all girls. *Submitted by Peggy Huner, daughter of Peter and Hazel Jacobs.*

45

ON THE ROAD AGAIN.
The Willys Overland Road Testing Team left their vehicles to pose for this circa 1914 photograph. Emil Hrbac, Sr. is the fourth man from the left. *Submitted by Susan Shaneck and Emily Fluhrer, granddaughters of Emil Hrbac, Sr.*

JUST US GIRLS.
Young mother, Kate Reno (seated), holds her daughter, Bessie, as her sister, Ada Shaneck, stands nearby. This female-only photo was taken early in 1913. *Submitted by Shirley Reynolds, daughter of Bessie, granddaughter of Kate, and niece of Ada.*

SPECIAL DELIVERY

United States Postal Service employees proudly pose at Toledo's Central Post 'Office on Thirteenth Street between Jefferson and Madison avenues. Though this photograph is undated, the building was built from 1909 to 1911 and designed to resemble the classic Treasury Building in Washington. *Submitted by Postmaster, Toledo, Ohio.*

AUTOMOBILE BUILDERS.

Taking time out for a picture is this team of auto workers. According to documentation on the photograph itself, this the "Final Assembly, Department 10, Willys Overland Auto Co., Toledo, O. Feb.-9-1912." The second gentleman from the right, with a moustache and both hands on his bib straps, is Fred J. Trost. *Submitted by Carlene Trost, granddaughter-in-law of Fred J. Trost.*

LADY BARBER.

The J. E. Miller and Son Barber Shop and College, located in the Colorado Building at 617 North St. Clair Street near Cherry Street, was one of the city's largest, with at least a dozen barbers in the years just before World War I. This photograph shows a group of apprentices, that includes a lady—unusual for that time. Times were changing, though, as the window advertisement for the Arcade Theatre (just up the street) shows; "Great Suffragettes Review, All Girls, etc." At Miller's, in 1914, one could get a haircut for ten cents, a shave for five cents, a massage or shampoo for ten cents or have a razor sharpened for fifteen cents. *Submitted by and caption written by Ken Levin.*

PRINTER'S INK.

Robert Oatley was the owner of the Commercial Printing Company at Monroe and Eleventh Streets. The young man, in the center of this August, 1914 photograph, is Nick Tanber. Young Nick is shown here working at his first job. He went on to work for The Toledo Blade for fifty years. *Submitted by Patt Camp, daughter of Nick Tanber.*

BEFORE WESTGATE.

Lena and August Schetter pose with their children Emma, Minnie, Frank, and George in 1915. Built in 1898, their home was on Central Avenue, near Secor Road, the future site of Westgate Village Shopping Center. *Submitted by Margie Ainsworth.*

BIRMINGHAM PARADE. This parade is proceeding down Genesee Street and approaching Consaul Street and St. Stephen's Catholic Church in the heart of Toledo's Hungarian neighborhood of Birmingham. Although not identified, this photograph may be of the celebration of the dedication of the third St. Stephen's Church building on August 23, 1914. This church building is still serving the neighborhood. Three priests are riding in the open car on what appears to be a hot summer day. The neighborhood used parades to celebrate other occasions, such as St. Stephen's Day and Hungarian Independence Day, as well. The right corner in the foreground is the present site of the Kinsey Funeral Home. The first building to the left is presently Tucker's Tavern and the rectangular brick building to its right is the former Palladium. Front Street factories can be seen at the top of the picture. *Submitted by Betty Holub, lifelong Birmingham resident.*

STACKED SHOES.

William Francis Barrett, far right, opened his first shoe store in East Toledo in 1898. After acquiring a second shoe business, and opening yet another, he combined the three into this large store, located at 135 Main Street. Also shown in this 1914 photograph are his sons, Lawrence Ross Barrett (on the left) and Charles Clifford Barrett. Lawrence and another brother, Tyler, continued operation of this store, along with their mother, May Barrett, after their father's death. Clifford later opened a Barrett Shoe Store in Wauseon. Barrett's was a fixture on Main Street in East Toledo for more that 77 years. *Submitted by Judy Lebowsky Shook.*

GRAND PIANO SALE.

Adam E. Kusian, the namesake of the A.E. Kusian Piano Company, is the gentleman on the left of the group in the foreground. His son, James Warner Kusian, is sitting on a piano crate in this remarkably sharp circa 1914 photograph. The pianos are lined up outside the Kusian store at 313-315 Main Street in East Toledo. The Art Furniture Company is next door in an area that abounds with advertising. Adam E. Kusian was the first Mayor of Walbridge, Ohio, an office he held for nine years. *Submitted by Mary J. Finch, daughter of James Warner Kusian and granddaughter of Adam E. Kusian.*

TOLEDO'S FIRST MOUNTED

Toledo's first mounted patrol was formed in 1908 and is shown here circa 1915 in front of the Toledo Museum of Art on Monroe Street. The officers are Merle Unkle, "Buck" Dear, Harry Sherfield, Bill Debren, Sergeant Jim Brittson, Joe Harrison, "Buck" Welsh, Cliff McClusky, and Chris Brenman. Each officer was required to provide care, which included feeding, cleaning and grooming, for his horse. This unit remained operational until 1928. The mounted patrol was revived by Chief John Mason in 1985 and remains active to this day. *Submitted by Matthew Beach.*

52

SUNDAY AFTERNOON AT THE HOFFMAN'S.

Anna and Christian Hoffman are seated in the back row center on the porch of their Walbridge Avenue home in the spring of 1915. They are surrounded by their children. Seated in the foreground are daughters Celia (left) and Mary. Brothers, from the left, are: Martin, Francis, George, and Joseph. *Submitted by Harold Hoffman, son of George Hoffman.*

BEFORE TRAFFIC LIGHTS.

Traffic Officer, Ray E. Allen directs drivers at the busy Madison Avenue and St. Clair Street intersection circa 1914. To the left is the famous Boody House Hotel, while the Nasby Building rises high in the background. Many of the buildings, seen looking west on Madison Avenue, are still in use. Officer Allen advanced through the ranks of the Toledo Police Department and became its Chief in 1936. In all, he served 42 years, 20 of them as Chief of Police. During his noteworthy career, he was responsible for the creation of the Scientific Crime Laboratory, the Police Academy, the Crime Prevention Squad, the Accident Investigation Unit, and the Harbor Patrol. He also developed the first radio patrol wagon, making the City of Toledo the first in the nation to utilize this concept. *Submitted by Carolyn Owens, Barbara McAllister, and Cindy Urbanus, granddaughters of Ray E. Allen.*

53

NOTABLE INTERSECTION.

Signs of change are apparent in George Sheperd's Livery sign on the corner post advertising "stables, feed and auto service" circa 1922. Interurban tracks round the corner (on the lower left). A wagon and a team of horses can be seen in the background and an automobile is parked on the right side of Wayne Street in Maumee. A group of young boys play in the center of town under the first, and only, electric street light. The Union Deposit Bank, built in 1888 in the popular Italianate style, and once a Lamsons Department Store, dominates the northwest corner. This historic building, like many of its neighbors, continues to serve the retail needs of the community in the Maumee Uptown Historic District and is on the National Register of Historic Places. *Submitted by Jack Hiles. Caption written by Marilyn Wendler.*

SCREAM FOR ICE CREAM.

A group of young men formed for this photograph on Tenth Street, between Adams and Jackson streets circa 1907. About half of the group is enjoying an ice cream cone. This photograph may have been taken by one of their own as the owner of this image believes that these are camera club members. The Peerless Knitting Mills Company was at the corner of Jackson and Tenth streets from 1906 to 1907. The building remains in use today. *Submitted by Robert Morris.*

54

CLASSY.

John J. Huebner proudly poses in his White touring car, parked crosswise on Ontario Street. Adams Street and the Lucas County courthouse provide the background for this early 20th century photograph. The courthouse was dedicated in 1897. The statue of President William McKinley was unveiled in 1903. Mr. Huebner was the eldest son of John and Catherine Huebner. He graduated from Stautzenberger Business College and received a degree of Master Brewer from the Chicago Brewmaster School. He was secretary-treasurer of the Huebner-Toledo Breweries Company, established by his father in 1905. When Prohibition forced the closing of the brewery operations in 1919, John J. Huebner went into the insurance business and formed the Huebner-Cavanaugh Insurance Company with offices at 225 Superior Street. *Submitted by Joan E. Moomey. Caption written by Fred Folger.*

FAMILY FARM.

This view shows the large barn and buildings on the Huebner farm. John Huebner, prominent Toledo brewer, bought this farm property on River Road near Waterville. Here, in 1902, he built a spacious red brick house for his future retirement. Those plans ended with his death in 1910. It served as a summer home for the family. Only the house remains at the present time. *Submitted by Joan E. Moomey. Caption written by Fred Folger.*

WAGONLOAD OF BEER.

This wagon is loaded with beer for delivery to various Toledo bars and saloons. The brewery was located on Hamilton Street and Swan Creek. It was an all day run for the horse-drawn shays to deliver barrels of beer, as far out as Secor Road and Monroe Street and to Wernert Corners at Douglas, Laskey, and Tremainsville roads. For some customers, the brewery not only supplied beer, but also pewter-topped mugs, metal trays with Huebner advertising, and even furniture. Peter Lenk originally established the brewery at this location. In 1882, it was incorporated as the Toledo Brewing and Malting Company. In 1896, John Huebner, in association with J.E. Pilliod, acquired ownership of brewing plant and changed the name to the Huebner Brewing Company. In 1902, they absorbed the Schmitt Brewing and Maumee Brewing companies. In 1905, they merged with the Grasser and Brand Breweries and Finlay Brewing Company. The expanded business was named the Huebner-Toledo Brewing Company. In 1919, Prohibition brought an end to this major Toledo enterprise. *Submitted by Joan E. Moomey. Caption written by Fred Folger.*

READY TO SLICE.

Peter Szuwart sharpens his knife prior to some meat cutting. His wife, Mary, is at his side at their 3139 Warsaw Street grocery store sometime in 1920. The others are most likely customers. The following year, the Szuwart's were involved in what was described as a "reign of terror" by The Toledo Blade. The newspaper reported, "…five holdups within an hour which culminated in the shooting of Peter Szuwart, grocer….A bullet was lodged in Mr. Szuwart's spine, but he recovered and continued in the grocery business. The perpetrators of the crime spree were apprehended. *Submitted by Theresa Nesbitt, daughter of Peter and Mary Szuwart.*

WILD AND CRAZY GUYS.

Ernest Robinson, third from the left, and his cousins go all out for Halloween, 1915. Clowning with him are, from the left, Zell Scott, Earl Scott, and Ferl Scott. *Submitted by Donna DeVerna, niece of Ernest Robinson.*

57

DIAMOND THEATRE, 1620-22 BROADWAY, TOLEDO, O.

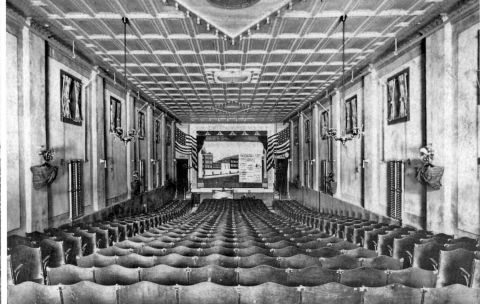

A ROOM WITH A VIEW.

The beautiful Diamond Theatre at 1520 (address on photograph is incorrect) Broadway in Toledo advertised why you should spend your evenings at their movie house which opened in 1910:

- It is the only theatre in the city built especially for motion pictures.
- Is modern and up-to-date in every detail with rest rooms for ladies and children.
- Is perfectly safe, fireproof, well-ventilated and lighted, equipped with the most modern cooling and heating appliances.
- Has concrete floor, insuring perfect sanitation.
- Our pictures are the finest and first shown in the South End; changed daily.
- Our Vaudeville and Pictures are clean, instructive and entertaining.
- Our orchestra music and singing are of the highest class.
- All can see, as there is a six-foot incline to stage.
- We employ only gentlemen, thus insuring courteous treatment to all.
- Come and be convinced.

Submitted by Don Noethen.

COOKING WITH KILOWATTS.

Grace Schreiber prepares a roast and potato dinner on her new electric stove circa 1916. Grace and her husband, Emmett, lived at 1725 Gilbert Road. *Submitted by Gregory and Patricia Rumer. Gregory is a grandson of Grace Schreiber.*

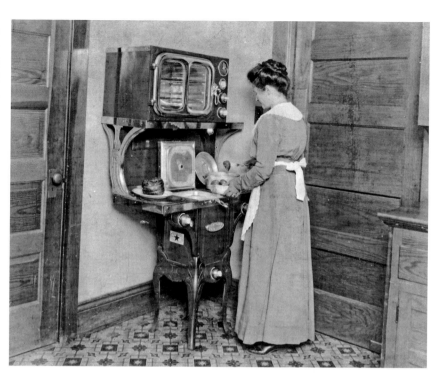

A BIG UNDERTAKING.

Elvin B. Wanzo established one of the first black-owned funeral homes in Toledo at 1412 Monroe Street in June, 1911. In business for 40 years, Mr. Wanzo moved three times before settling at 572 Nebraska Avenue in 1937. He retired ten years later, and sold the business to an employee, Clarence "Jack" Dale. *Submitted by Sheryl A. Riggs, Managing Director, Dale-Riggs Funeral Home, Inc.*

BUSIER NOW.

This quiet slice of life in South Toledo is at the corner of Wildwood Road and Glendale Avenue, near the Anthony Wayne Trail circa 1915. It's hard to imagine that this now busy intersection was once so peaceful and quiet. *Submitted by Gregory and Patricia Rumer.*

WHERE'S THE FIRE?
This photograph was taken in front of the Lucas County National Guard Armory on Spielbusch Avenue circa 1915. Several pieces of Toledo Fire Department apparatus are shown after they were converted from horse-drawn to motorized vehicles in 1915. Part of the building, which was located on the current site of the Federal courthouse, was also temporarily used as a fire station in 1918. This move was forced when the wall and foundation of the Number 3, or headquarters station, at Jefferson and Ontario streets began to collapse and had to be rebuilt. Ironically, this magnificent structure and landmark was destroyed in a spectacular fire December 21, 1934. *Submitted by the Toledo Firefighters Museum. Caption written by Tim Boaden, Department Historian.*

BRIDGE FIX.

Workers replace the brick roadway on the Ash-Consaul Bridge over the Maumee River circa 1940. Shown here is the west, or Ash Street, end of the bridge. The bridge linked near-north Toledo to the Birmingham neighborhood from 1913 to 1957. Much of the support steel used to construct it, had been originally been a part of the Cherry Street Bridge, built in 1884. Business signs for the Beebe Fuel Company and Karavan Coffee suggest this photograph is circa 1940. It is also known that there was a 1940 Works Progress Administration (WPA) project to improve the bridge and its approaches. *Submitted by Sharon Yaros.*

ADULTS ONLY PLEASE.

Young Raymond Gable peeks out the window at 1020 Klondike Street as his mother, Helen Gable (in the white blouse), her sister, Lillian Durbin (center front), and friends pose in 1916. *Submitted by Marjorie Scalia, granddaughter of Helen, daughter of Raymond.*

BRIDGE WALK.

Henry G. Sartor takes a walk across the Maumee River on the Cherry Street Bridge in 1916. Mr. Sartor is walking toward East Toledo while a large horse-drawn wagon passes him in the opposite direction. *Submitted by Bernard H. Sartor, son of Henry G. Sartor.*

WEIGHING IN.

Joseph D. Roberts stands before his store at 2944 Monroe Street on April 27, 1916. Mr. Roberts' advertisement in the Toledo city directory listed his business as "Dealer in coal, coke, wood, flour, feed, grain, hay, straw, and chicken feed. Also hay and straw wholesale. Baggage express delivery." The driver of the horse-drawn wagon has paused on an in-ground platform scale. The scale manufacturer displays its name at the corner of the building – Fairbanks. *Submitted by Doris Roberts, daughter-in-law of Joseph D. Roberts.*

63

ROW, ROW, ROW YOUR BOAT.

The Sommers sisters take to the water at Put-In-Bay, Ohio during the summer of 1917. In the cardboard dinghy are; Helen Sommers Fazekas, Lena Sommers Hunter, Myrtle Sommers Maher, and Ruth Sommers Shinevar. *Submitted by Suzanne Dial, daughter of Myrtle Sommers Maher.*

HANDLE WITH CARE.

Clarence "Jimmie" Shabnow, 18, is shown here as a truck driver for the Ohio Plate & Window Glass Company in 1916. The company was located at 313-319 Morris Street. Note that the glass on the truck bed was well-packed as, the truck had hard rubber tires. So, the ride over the stone road and rails was rough. Pneumatic tires were available, but not yet dependable. *Submitted by Ed Shabnow.*

64

TIME TO RELAX.

A St. Agnes School picnic at Ottawa Park was enjoyed by all these girls in 1917. Seated are; Charlotte Daunhauer, Dorothy Miller, and Madaline LeDua. In the back row are; Leona Matz, Helen Tollman, Julianna Hope, and Gertrude Daunhauer. *Submitted by Fr. Dan Fraser, former pastor of St. Agnes Church*

DIRT ROAD.

Alton Delbert Barhite is driving the wagon while Herb Johnson tends the pair of horses to his right. The identity of the others is not known. Avondale Avenue was not paved when this photograph was taken in 1918. *Submitted by Pat Anaszewicz, granddaughter of Alton Delbert Barhite.*

65

INTERMISSION.

Abram Ruvinsky played violin for the Toledo Railways and Light Company's Orchestra. He was a native of Kiev, Russia, and came to Toledo in 1910. This photograph was taken on August 10, 1917. *Submitted by Susan Morel.*

HIGH HAND STAND.

Robert T. "Tom" Morris does a handstand for the camera high above Michigan Street, between Adams and Jackson streets, in downtown Toledo circa 1916. Mr. Morris was the Assistant Physical Director at the Young Men's Christian Association (YMCA) and used the roof of the "Y's" building to demonstrate his physical fitness. When he wasn't standing on his hands, he taught gym and swimming for boys. *Submitted by Robert Morris, son of Robert T. "Tom" Morris.*

BANK BUILDER.

Bertrand D. Roadarmel, wearing the white shirt, poses with this Herman Suhrbier Company crew circa 1919. Mr. Roadarmel was foreman and timekeeper for the construction company. The men are building a bank at the northwest corner of Lagrange Street and Central Avenue. This was his first Toledo employment, having moved here from Haskins, Ohio. Their work was lasting, as the building still stands in the heart of the Polish Village. *Submitted by Hollis Sobb, granddaughter of Bertrand D. Roadarmel.*

A STROLL WITH THE KIDS.

Irene Alice Rawlings is out for a stroll on Page Street with her favorite dolls in the early spring of 1919. *Submitted by Janet Scott, granddaughter of Irene Alice Rawlings Eyne.*

LOAD OF TANKS.

Alton Delbert Barhite is on the left of this wagon, loaded with water tanks in this circa 1920 photograph. The American Plumbers Supply was at 618 Jackson Street. Listings in the Toledo city directory show that Mr. Barhite worked as a teamster. *Submitted by Pat Anaszewicz, granddaughter of Alton Delbert Barhite.*

BOAT HAULING.

Alton Delbert Barhite is the third from the left as this boat-hauling crew pauses for this circa 1920 photograph. The scene is most likely the busy lumber handling area along Swan Creek and the Miami and Erie Canal. *Submitted by Pat Anaszewicz, granddaughter of Alton Delbert Barhite.*

ANGELS IN THE YARD.

The West sisters, Florence (5) and Helen (2), look almost angelic while picking flowers in the backyard of their home in the 100 block of Western Avenue in the spring of 1920. *Submitted by Karen Miller, granddaughter of Florence West.*

THE INTERURBAN ERA.

Toledo was a hub for a number of electric-powered inter-urban railroads which appear-ed about 1900. This type of public trans-portation con-nected cities with the sub-urbs, rural areas and communi-ties, and other nearby cities. Interurban cars

were generally larger than city streetcars, such as the Detroit-Monroe-Toledo Car #510, pic-tured here. In the open country, some were capable of fast speeds, up to 80 mph. They offered frequent schedules, running every one or two hours. This allowed rural dwellers to commute to the city for work, shopping, and entertainment. Some lines had electric locomo-tives for freight service outside the city. These railroads had their own rights of way and tracks with the necessary overhead power wires. Once the passenger interurbans reached the city, they shared the rails and power of the city streetcar system. Most local interurban routes con-verged on Superior Street, near Jackson Street, in Toledo. This was the location of the down-town interurban passenger station, also pictured here. Passengers boarded from both sides of Superior Street. Among the lines that served Toledo were: The Toledo & Western, a route that went to Pioneer, via Sylvania, with a branch to Adrian. The Toledo & Indiana, a route that went as far as Bryan. The Toledo, Bowling Green & Southern. The Toledo, Fostoria, & Findlay. The Toledo, Maumee, & Perrysburg. The Ohio Public Service, a route that extend-ed east as far as Marblehead via Elmore and Port Clinton. The Lakeshore Electric served Toledo and Cleveland via Fremont and Sandusky. The Cincinnati & Lake Erie connected Toledo with Cincinnati via Dayton and Lima. The interurban era ended in the early 1930s – a victim of affordable automobiles and the Great Depression. *Submitted by Ross Goodfellow. Caption written by Fred Folger.*

PAIR OF PARASOLS.

These two couples enjoy each other's company and a pleasant day in the outdoors. On the left are Charles P. and Alma Q. Pappenfus. The second couple is Ernest and Louise Helmer Quetschke. Ernest and Alma were siblings. This photograph was taken, circa 1919, on the beautiful grounds of The Toledo State Hospital. *Submitted by Shirley Pawlowski, granddaughter of Ernest and Louise Helmer Quetschke.*

CHIP DELIVERY.

Burt E. LaLonde is dressed for cold weather, as he stands on his truck's running board circa 1930. Mr. LaLonde worked for Kuehmann's as a salesman of their snack food products for 33 years. *Submitted by Carol Cahoo, granddaughter of Burt E. LaLonde.*

HISTORICAL PRAISES.

Fifteen North Erie Street, between Washington and Monroe streets, was the second home of Northwest Ohio's oldest African Methodist Episcopal Church, Warren A.M.E Church. Founded in 1847, Warren A.M.E. continues to fill the pews at its current location, 915 Collingwood Boulevard at Indiana Avenue. *Submitted by Gloria D. Johnston, member of Warren A.M.E.Church.*

PACKING PLACE.

This is the Jacob Folger Packing House, located at 500 Phillips Avenue. Jacob Folger, a native of Bavaria, opened his first butcher shop on Washington Street at age 20. As business increased, he subsequently moved to two successive locations on St. Clair Street. In 1883, he purchased a tract of land on Phillips Avenue, along the railroad, in West Toledo. Here, he consolidated the slaughtering operation and processing of quality hams, bacon, and sausage products. The plant would be expanded several times after this circa 1900 photograph. For a time, it was the largest meat packing company in northwest Ohio. In 1958, after 94 years, merchandising trends caused the closing of the company. The buildings were razed in 1965. Well before the century's end, no Toledo meat packing companies remained in business. *Submitted by Jerry Moore. Caption written by Fred Folger.*

MOVIE TIME.

The Victory Theatre opened at 412 Adams Street, between Superior and St. Clair streets in 1908. Movies were continuous and admission was five cents. Featured the day this photograph was taken were, In Old Tennessee, a drama, and a cowboy comedy, Percy and His Squaw. *Submitted by Hollis Sobb.*

TICKETS PLEASE.

Miss Nellie Dushane takes a break from ticket selling for this photograph. She was a cashier at the Victory Theatre from 1914 to 1916. *Submitted by Dale F. Beaudry, nephew of Nellie Dushane.*

RIDING HIGH.

William J. Rockefeller (a cousin of John D. Rockefeller) was a greens-keeper extraordinaire at the Inverness Club. He began at the club when it opened in 1903. And over the course of his tenure, Inverness developed into a magnificent championship golf course. According to the United States Golf Association in 1922, "Every inch of the course [Inverness] was built by him; and he has brought it along through several reconstructions, to its present place as one of the great courses in the country…." As the golf course superintendent, he was charged with the responsibility of getting the course into first-class condition for the 1920 United States Open Championship. Mr. Rockefeller often traveled and worked with others in improving golf courses and designed a number of Ohio courses himself. As shown here, circa 1920, he often used a horse to assist him in getting around the course for inspection and supervision purposes. *Submitted by Greg Fish.*

OVERLAND BEAUTIES.

Marie Louise Schuchman is sitting on the running board, along with her fellow Willys Overland secretaries in the fall of 1922. They pose with a company-produced automobile. An advertising agency recruited the ladies at the plant, outfitted them, and photographed them around the new car. The ladies were compensated with lunch at a country club, the rest of the day off, and five dollars. *Submitted by Charles James Gillespie, Jr., son of Louise Schuchman Gillespie.*

73

HOT TOMATO.

Edward B. Wright, Sr. drives a company truck that bears his name circa 1915. He established the Wright Brothers Wholesale Gardeners along with his brother, Arthur, in 1915. The company was located on West Bancroft Street across the street from the site which, in 1931, became, and remains, the campus of the University of Toledo. The enterprise continued into the 1960s when it had 13 acres of greenhouses growing two crops of hothouse tomatoes each year. *Submitted by Kevin Kubiak, great-grandson of Edward B. Wright.*

COME SIT A SPELL.

Maggie Banks, standing, and her sister, Elizabeth Enty, top right, enjoy an afternoon visit with neighbors on the front porch of her Pinewood Avenue home in September, 1924. *Submitted by Calvin Banks, Sr., grandson of Maggie Banks.*

AMBULANCE.

Miss Geneva Reed stands in front of a J.R. Clegg ambulance in the early 1920s. The Toledo city directory listing for 1924 described Clegg's complete services; "James R. Clegg Funeral Parlors, Funeral Directors, Undertakers & Embalmers, Ambulance and Funeral Car Service." The mortuary was located at 910 Starr Avenue in East Toledo.
Submitted by Patricia Gladfelter.

CORNER DRUGSTORE.

David S. Schweitzer was proprietor of the Collingwood Pharmacy for more than 26 years, beginning in 1906. He was also Clerk-In-Charge of the United States Post Office (Toledo Station Number 14), located inside his store at Monroe Street and Collingwood Boulevard. The posing horse and driver both work for the Toledo Ice Delivery Company which employed more than 150 people and operated five distributing stations in different parts of the city. The company handled both ice manufactured from distilled and filtered water and pure crystal ice from Whitmore Lake, Michigan. In total, The Toledo Ice Delivery Company handled over 50,000 tons of ice annually, about half of Toledo's usage. The company also handled coal and had offices at 1150 Elm Street. *Submitted by Ed Shabnow.*

NEIGHBORHOOD SOCIAL CENTER.

John William King Albright stands in front of The Cash Corner Store in 1921 (photograph on the left). His son, Carl R. Albright, and Carl's wife, Elizabeth Coleman Albright (shown in the photograph on the right), operated the store at 1700 Indiana Avenue and reared eight children in the grocery building. Carl was also employed at Champion Spark Plug from 1915 until 1935. Elizabeth, born in Scotland, looked quite capable of handling a husband, store, home, and a large brood of children. *Submitted by John Binns Albright, grandson of Carl and Elizabeth Albright.*

HUNGARIAN FUNERAL.

The Hungarian tradition of bringing the remains of the deceased back to the family home continued in America until the 1940s. Shown here is the funeral of John Masney, Sr., of Payne Avenue, in the Birmingham neighborhood, circa 1921. Sometimes a photograph was taken at the home or the casket was reopened at the cemetery.

Following this photo session, the casket was closed and the procession to the cemetery began. These pictures were often sent back to Hungary, some say, to show that the deceased relative or friend had a beautiful funeral. The picture-taking tradition stopped around 1930. *Submitted by Margaret Fern.*

Memories are important at Mancy's

Although just a few are likely to recall the original Ideal Restaurant as it was founded by Gus Mancy and his cousin, Nicholas Graham in 1921, hopefully more will remember the Mancy's that grew from a small eating spot on Phillips Avenue at the end of the trolley line into the restaurant which just celebrated 84 continuous years in business.

In August 1973, the original Mancy's was completely destroyed by fire. Nothing remained... nothing but the memories, however.

The original Mancy's would never be duplicated, but the memory of it all and its commitment to preserving something of the past remains.

The family's love and understanding of outstanding food and hospitality has been passed down through three generations to be enjoyed by many customers to come.

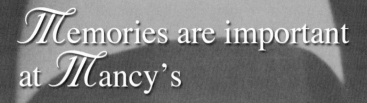

Menu from 1939

Menu
Ideal Restaurant
and Cocktail Bar
938-937 Phillips Avenue
WEST TOLEDO

May We Suggest
Ideal Special STEAK SANDWICH
On Toast
French Fried Potatoes
Tomato and Pickle
30 c

TRY OUR
LOUISIANA FRESH SHRIMP COCKTAIL
25 c

SPECIAL
BROILED SIRLOIN STEAK
Hashed Brown Potatoes
Head Lettuce and French Dressing
Coffee, Tea or Milk
85 c

OUR FAMOUS
HAMBURGER DeLUXE
French Fried Potatoes
Tomato and Pickle
20 c

HOT ROAST PORK OR BEEF SANDWICHES With Potatoes and Gravy **25 c**

BEEF TENDERLOIN STEAK
FRENCH FRIED POTATOES — HEAD LETTUCE AND TOMATO SALAD
COFFEE, TEA OR MILK
75 ¢

Ideal RESTAURANT

MANCY'S IDE

John and George 1968

eef Tenderloin STEAK SANDWICH ON TOAST

Gus Mancy 21 Years Old 1919

Committed to preserving the past while moving towards the future.

MANCY'S STEAKS ESTABLISHED IN 1921

953 Phillips Avenue
Toledo 419·476·4154

A PRETTY PICKLE

Three kinds of pickles are front and center in this display of goods at the Thrift Grocery Company store at 1759 North Erie Street at the corner of Ash Street circa 1922. Thrift operated a chain of stores throughout the city. Norma Ashmann is the young girl in the middle. She is flanked by her Aunt Mathelda Bartleheim and her older sister, Alvina Ashmann, along with neighbor, Fred Nachtman. All lived nearby on Erie Street. The grocer's identity is not known. *Submitted by Norma Ashmann Ethington.*

DARBY GIRL.

Florence West , third row from the right and fourth seat from the rear, and her classmates sit at attention. Mrs. Gilday's is their first grade teacher at Immaculate Conception School at Eastern and Crittenden avenues in the fall of 1922. The school was affectionately called "The Darby" by the community. *Submitted by Larry Barhite, son of Florence West.*

NEW TRUCK.

Howard N. Warner loads a new delivery truck from his 602 Dixie Highway grocery store in Rossford circa 1921. The Dixie Highway may muddy his whitewall tires. Warner had previously been an optometrist and had run a dairy delivery operation (see pages 27 and 34). *Submitted by Nancy Stonerock, granddaughter of Howard N. Warner.*

79

PORTRAIT OF DISTINCTION.
Loretta McAleese is pictured here for her high school graduation in June, 1922. Now, as Loretta McAleese Bauer, she is set apart from her classmates as she is, at 100 years of age, the oldest living alumna of the Notre Dame Academy. *Submitted by Carol Bauer Zilba, daughter of Loretta McAleese Bauer.*

TRUCKLOAD OF BAGS.
Lloyd M. Renschler is behind the wheel of this loaded truck in 1922. Mr. Renschler worked many years for the G.E. Conkey Company which was located on Nebraska Avenue between Collingwood Boulevard and Erie Street. The company processed and packaged animal feed, cornmeal, and flour which it distributed in Toledo and its surrounding communities. *Submitted by Kathryn Strand, daughter of Lloyd M. Renschler.*

SMOKING SECTION.
Fred Kirdahy, on the left, and John Kirdahy, take an afternoon break in fall of 1922. The scene is outside of John's Tailor and Dry Cleaner at 1111 Adams Street. *Submitted by Tatiana Kirdahy, daughter-in-law of John Kirdahy.*

BABY BLUES.

Olive Hyott is clearly upset as she plays with her sister, Lorna Hyott. Neither sister is sure why Olive was in tears circa 1923. *Submitted by sisters Olive Hyott Zilba and Lorna Hyott Haines.*

FLOWERS ON THE GO.

Albert Lehmann drives one of the early delivery trucks utilized by Schramm Brothers Flowers. The company's store at 1307-1315 Cherry Street is shown here with patriotic decorations circa 1922. Peering out of the window are George and Frank Schramm. *Submitted by Mary Beth Schramm Garbe, granddaughter of Frank Schramm.*

YOUR TABLE IS READY.

Herman C. Greiner holds the door open at his restaurant and café circa 1916. Mr. Greiner's establishment was located at 102-104 Summit Street and was described in the Toledo city directory as; "Dealer in Imported & Domestic Wines & Liquors. First-Class Restaurant In Connection." *Submitted by Viola C. Fabian, niece of Herman C. Greiner.*

SELF PORTRAIT.

Photographer O.L. McDonald took this spectacular photograph of the west side of Superior Street between Locust Street (on the left) and Lagrange Street circa 1921. Mr. McDonald lived at 913 Superior Street, the third house from the left. His next door neighbor, on his right, was Mary Ardner at 907 Superior, built in 1860. All the houses in this entire block are still standing. Their neighborhood is described on a nearby plaque placed by the Toledo Sesquicentennial Commission, "The pioneer Village of Vistula is now bounded by Walnut, Champlain, Chestnut, Magnolia, and Summit Streets. Established in 1833 by Benjamin F. Stickney and Edward Bissell, Vistula was merged with its rival, Port Lawrence, and in 1837 both villages were incorporated as Toledo. The Vistula Historic District, Toledo's oldest neighborhood, was listed on the National Register of Historic Places in 1978." *Submitted by Carol Ardner, granddaughter of Mary Ardner.*

SUNDAY BEST.

Mrs. Esther Shoecraft Allen was born in Toledo at 1855 Ontario Street to Alice and John Shoecraft. She is pictured here, in 1924, with three of the six children she had with her husband Guy Allen. From the left the children are, James, William, and Alice. The couple's family grew with the births of Charles, Joseph and Mabel. Guy and Esther were believed to be the first black family to own their home on Mayo Street in North Toledo. The Allen's were members of Warren A.M.E. Church. *Submitted by Charles D. and Elinor W. Allen, son and daughter-in-law of Esther Shoecraft Allen.*

CORNER MARKET.

Steve Werkman's Meat Market, shown here, circa 1928, featured Hungarian sausage which was made fresh daily. Werkman's was in stall #87 in the Summit and Cherry Market. The market opened in 1917 in a four-story structure at Summit and Cherry streets that had been built in 1882. The market had an international flavor and flourished until the depression and World War II caused business to slacken. Most of the retails shops closed by the 1950s and the building was razed in 1968. A portion of One Seagate now occupies the site. John Grigsby wrote in The Blade in 1990, "The Summit-Cherry Market was an early version of today's shopping mall, with more than 40 separate and independent entrepreneurs operating shops under one roof." *Submitted by Stephen Werkman, son of Steve Werkman.*

WAITE STANDOUT.

Waite High School's Leonard F. "Duke" Reilly was proclaimed "one of the finest athletes the school has ever turned out" by the Toledo Blade in 1924 and Waite Coach, Larry Bevan, credited his big center for making "Waite football famous the country over." Duke , who also was the catcher for Waite's city championship baseball team, went on to play football at Toledo University. He was later successful in Toledo business, too, as he was a partner of the Reilly-Wearley Company, an automobile dealership. *Submitted by Jack Reilly, grandson of Leonard F. "Duke" Reilly.*

HEAD AND SHOULDERS ABOVE THE REST.

Mrs. Lydia Broughton's millinery shop made and provided hatwear for ladies. She operated this store at 646 Main Street in East Toledo from 1919 until 1925. The interior photograph shows Hazel Delauter Dicken, on the left, and Mrs. Lydia Broughton on right. It is Mrs. Broughton in the exterior photograph. After learning the trade here, Hazel Delauter Dicken later opened her own shop in the Spitzer Arcade.

Submitted by Millicent M. Apardian, niece of Hazel Delauter Dicken.

A WOMAN WITH A PLAN.

When Ella P. Stewart discovered there were no black-owned drugstores in Toledo, she and her husband William moved to the city and established Stewart's Pharmacy. This photograph, which shows Mrs. Stewart behind the counter, is a rare glimpse of the interior of the pharmacy, located at 566 Indiana and City Park avenues, circa 1923. Mrs. Stewart is believed to be the first African-American woman licensed to practice pharmacy in the United States. *Submitted by Ella P. Stewart Collection, The Center for Archival Collections, Bowling Green State University.*

OPEN FOR BUSINESS.

Ella P. Stewart opens Stewart's Pharmacy for the day on a morning in the early 1940s. The civic-minded Mrs. Stewart worked to improve living conditions for black families. Her efforts thrust her to national and international prominence and lead to her service as a United Nations Goodwill Ambassador. In 1961, Ella P. Stewart Elementary School was named in her honor. The school is now known as the Ella P. Stewart Academy for Girls. *Submitted by Ella P. Stewart Collection, The Center for Archival Collections, Bowling Green State University.*

A HANDSOME HEARSE.

A Coyle Funeral Home hearse is parked at Saints Peter and Paul Catholic Church on South St. Clair Street circa 1925. The Coyle Funeral Home was founded in 1888 by Lucas County Commissioner and Masons and Bricklayers Union President, James Coyle, a native of Ireland. The company first located on Broadway, near downtown Toledo (see page 26). The funeral home passed on to his son, William, and then, to his grandsons, William and James. Today, the firm is operated by great-grandsons, William and Joseph Coyle. *Submitted by Joseph Coyle, great-grandson of James Coyle.*

THE BLADE GIRLS.

According to these ladies, The Blade is "First in Toledo." Erma Fletcher is in the middle of the line in this circa 1925 photograph. She was a member of a dance troupe and a tap dance teacher in Toledo. *Submitted by Bill LaPountney, nephew of Erma Fletcher.*

87

SUMMER RESPITE.

Madeline Hem and her children, Katherine, Paul, Clarice, and Halvor, Jr. (Duke) enjoy a day at Walbridge Park circa 1920s. Madeline's husband, Halvor Warren Hem, was Chief Design Engineer at the former Toledo Scale Company and known to many as "Mr. Scale." *Submitted by James Meredith, son of Clarice and grandson of Madeline Hem.*

MULTI-GROCER.

In the above right image, grocer, William Michael Post, is the third man from the left, wearing a cap and apron, circa 1925. In the photograph to the right, he is fourth from the left. Both these stores were on Dorr Street (above is 1316 Dorr Street and right is 1508-1512 Dorr Street). These were among the five stores he owned at one time. Mr. Post's once expanding enterprise was thwarted by the Great Depression and his grocery business was forced into bankruptcy. *Submitted by Marilyn Post Wiley, granddaughter of William Michael Post.*

MALE RITE OF PASSAGE.

Edward C. Royce and his brother, Ambro, enjoy stogies as they ride their bicycles in the north end of Toledo circa 1920s. Wheels were as important then, as they are now. Cigar smoking, however, is less socially acceptable among youth of today. *Submitted by Richard Royce.*

EARLY AERIAL PHOTOGRAPH.

The National Malleable Castings Company foundry, located between the Maumee River and Front Street is shown in this circa 1923 aerial photograph. The plant was demolished during the depression. The Birmingham neighborhood is across Front Street from the plant. Visible landmarks include the Number 13 Fire Station, Birmingham School, and the Western & Lake Erie RR tracks. *Submitted by Louis Visi.*

DRESSED FOR THE PART.

The Men's Club of Washington Congregational Church (Lawrence & West Woodruff) presents a play for the congregation in 1922. Allen Colby in seated in the front row, second from the right. *Submitted by Ann Weber, granddaughter of Allen Colby.*

MILK DELIVERY.

The Babcock Dairy Company's delivery trucks line up outside their Berdan Avenue offices and processing plant circa 1931. Babcock served retail stores and home delivery customers from this West Toledo location for many years. Babcock's motto was, "The Safe Milk for The Baby." The building still stands and the stack, as shown here, remains a local landmark. *Submitted by Sharon Yaros.*

Wayne — June 11 - '26 — Libby

AHHHHHH, SUMMER!

Roy Rehfeldt, third from right, second row, is happy to be graduating from the eighth grade. The celebration took place at Wayne School on Western Avenue and Airport Highway on June 11, 1926. *Submitted by Paul Reheldt.*

SAY (GOAT) CHEESE!

Trying to drum up business, traveling photographers would knock on doors with animals and wagons in tow. During the early 1900s, a beloved prop for youngsters was the goat-drawn cart. A photographer's animals could prove particularly thrilling to Toledo children, during the Great Depression. Adorable is the only description for this 1925 photo of Gilbert Wagoner, age three. *Submitted by Jean Wagoner, wife of Gilbert Wagoner.*

91

THE GREAT EXPANSION.
The A. Bentley and Sons Construction Company is in high gear, creating one of many expansions of the Electric Auto-Lite plant on Champlain Street. This photograph is dated April 2, 1926. *Submitted by Leonard Schultz.*

THIS PIGGY GOES TO MARKET.
Philip Provo, long-time Toledo meat market operator and sausage maker, stands in the door of his store at 3628 Monroe Street circa 1925. Mr. Provo and his new bride, Lena, came to Toledo from Germany in 1904. He established his business in 1908. Provo Meats proved to be a Toledo institution. Provo continually updated and modernized his store and sausage factory and made 21 different kinds of sausages. Philip Provo died in 1966 and family members carried on until 1972 – 64 years at the same location. *Submitted by Betty Provo Cochran, daughter of Philip Provo.*

HIGH CHARGE.

Clarence Sauer, on the left, and Charley Flint are at their work stations while a customer looks on. This photograph is of the interior of Flint & Mann at 106 Michigan Street and was taken June 10, 1926. The company serviced automotive batteries. *Submitted by Bonna Weaver, daughter of Clarence Sauer.*

SNAZZY CAR.

Albert R. Tucker, shown here sitting on the bumper of his first car in 1926, was believed to be the first deaf-mute in Toledo to receive a driver's license. He lived on Montrose Avenue. *Submitted by Donald and Arlene Wines. Donald is a grandson of Albert Tucker.*

FUTURE NINTH GRADERS.

This large 1926 Jones Junior High graduating class proudly holds its diplomas. Clyde Johnson, fifth from right, back row, is itching to remove his tie and begin the summer vacation. *Submitted by Judy Johnson Tunison, daughter of Clyde Johnson.*

94

FILL 'ER UP.

This pilot needs fuel and is ready to fill up at Crabb's filling station. Crabb's was at the southeast corner of Alexis and Telegraph roads when this photograph was taken in 1926. Shell gasoline was selling for 21 cents per gallon at the time. *Submitted by Charles Stahl.*

HAPPY NAME.

The Smile Baseball Club took to the Toledo sandlots in 1927. Most are smiling, but only a few are identified in this photograph. Harry Brubakers is kneeling, second from the right. Bob Kirk is on the far left in the back row with E.P. Young to his left. Continuing to the right, there is an unidentified player, Ed Hunter (middle of row), Scotty Alfrey, Mr. Smith, and, with the biggest smile of all, is manager, John Burdick. *Submitted by Jean Christy, daughter of Ed Hunter.*

95

BIKE GIVEAWAY.
Frank Poczekaj, owner of this Lagrange Street pharmacy, delighted some young child with this brand new bicycle. Neighborhood children, including Rosemarie Bohnsack, Frank's niece and the smallest girl pictured in front, happily gathered for this 1928 photo. St. Hedwig's Church is in the background to the left. *Submitted by Rosemarie Bohnsack.*

PICNIC BOUND.

Cliff Cooley, of 3018 Chase Street, proudly stands in front of his car, containing his wife, Mildred, daughter, Evelyn, mother, Lucinda, and father, Fred, in this 1928 photograph. The Cooleys are on their way to a picnic. *Submitted by Nancy Cooley, granddaugher-in-law of Cliff Cooley.*

THE BUGGY STOPS HERE.

Sisters Janet (left) and Nancy Maher, daughters of Paul and Myrtle Maher, walk their baby buggies down Bluff Street during the summer of 1927. *Submitted by Suzanne Dial, sister of Janet and Nancy Maher.*

LONG LASTING FAITH.

Established in 1868, the Third Baptist Church, pictured here in 1927, remains a cornerstone of the community at 402 Pinewood Avenue. *Submitted by Third Baptist Church*

STRIKE UP THE BAND.

The Frederick Douglass Community Center was organized on New Year's Day, 1919, by a group of ten men led by Albertus Brown. Mr. Brown, a lawyer and civic leader, was inspired by the need for social and recreational opportunities for the African-American youth of Toledo. The Center's namesake, Frederick Douglas, was born a slave in 1818 and became an American abolitionist, editor, author, statesman, and reformer. The Frederick Douglas Community Center's band of 1927 is shown here. The Center remains actively involved in the community at 1001 Indiana Avenue. *Submitted by the Frederick Douglass Community Association and Thomas Vines, Jr.*

WATER STREET WOODWORKERS.

The staff of the Western Manufacturing Company presented for this photograph in front of the company offices at 731 Walnut Street on August 16, 1928. The company, which incorporated in 1870, was a dealer in lumber and roofing materials, as well as manufacturers of doors, sash, screens, and other mill work. Their facilities stretched for two full blocks, from Vine to Sycamore, on Water Street and included a yard and factory. The company later changed its name to the Western Woodwork & Lumber Company and remained in business until 1958. Shown standing in the back row, 11th man from the left, is company Vice-President C.C.F. Sieving. To his left is President Fred J. Puck. Sitting immediately in front of the two officers is Shipping Clerk and Mechanic, Frank August Hinkleman. Hinkleman was a long-time employee and father of this picture's donor. *Submitted by Ralph Hinkleman, son of Frank Hinkleman.*

FOILED!

Seventeen-year-old Curtis Shepler, on the right, and his friend (unknown), are ready to race in June, 1928. At age 15, Curtis had shot at a burglar who was attempting to rob his mother's sweet shop on Ashland Avenue. *Submitted by Sandra Mattier, daughter of Curtis Shepler.*

A HOLY CELEBRATION.

The Slowinski family gathers to celebrate Florence Slowinski's (in white) first Holy Communion in 1929. Gathered in the yard at their 1209 Evesham home, from the left, are: Floyd Winkle, Cora Winkle, Joe Slowinski Leo Bas, Andy Slowinski, and Grandma Slowinski. Florence's siblings are Joe, Elonore and Bob Slowinski. *Submitted by Lisa Binkowski, daughter of Joe Binkowski.*

George Zientara

SOLEMN PROCESSION.

Police Officers, family, friends and neighbors observed the funeral procession for George Zientara, at his home, 1042 Tecumseh Street. Mr. Zientara was a Toledo Police Officer killed in the line of duty. He was shot at 2304 Upton Avenue by robbery suspects on April 16, 1928. Officer Zientara was appointed to the force in 1920 and is memorialized, along with his fellow fallen officers, at The Police Memorial Garden on Toledo's Civic Center Mall. *Submitted by Nancy Zientara Thabit.*

LESSONS IN THE PARK.

Bertha Stephens, seated far right, has a captive audience. Her daughter, Irma, is seated next to her and her son, Nash, is in the grey cap. They are with friends in Walbridge Park circa 1930. *Submitted by Bertha Coley, daughter of Irma, granddaughter of Bertha, and niece of Nash.*

NINETY-EIGHT STRONG.

It was a beautiful day, August 11, 1929, for ninety-eight members of the Schardt family who enjoyed a picnic and family reunion at Ottawa Park. Laura Schardt, fourth from left in the second row, married George Cousino in 1927. *Submitted by Larry and Carol Cousino, Larry is the son of Laura Schardt Cousino.*

TRANSPORTATION IN TRANSITION AND A GREAT STORE.

This view looks across the intersection Adams and Huron streets to the long-popular Lasalle & Koch Department Store. The automobile age was well-established by the time of this photo in 1929. Cars are parked at curbside and a Community Traction Company bus stops at the corner near the Huron Street revolving-door entrance to the store. Yet behind, we see a horse and buggy approaching. Also, we see the streetcar rails in the pavement and the overhead trolley wires. This was a busy intersection dominated by the large store and the Paramount Theater across Adams Street. Lasalle's moved into their new eight-story building in 1917. Ten years later, three more floors were added. There were nineteen display windows along Adams and Huron streets and eight elevators to transport customers to the various departments. The first floor's main aisle stretched the length of the store from the Adams entrance to the back where it connected with the popular arcade in the Spitzer Building. Shoppers eagerly sought bargains along the aisle. In 1981, the store took the name of it's parent company, Macy's. However, declining business brought the closing of this last of downtown Toledo's department stores in 1984. After being vacant for a number of years, the handsome commercial building has been successfully converted to residential apartments. *Submitted by the Toledo Area Regional Transit Authority (TARTA). Caption written by Fred Folger.*

POSEYS ON PARADE.

Allwin Schroeder (girls' identity unknown), son of Myrtle ImOberstag Schroeder, rides along in the cab of a Myrtle Flowers delivery truck, transformed into a parade float in August, 1929. Myrtle's love of flowers began as a young girl when she worked with her parents, owners of ImOberstag Greenhouse on Western Avenue. She established her shop in 1928 at 933 Dorr Street. Allwin operated the shop from the early 1950's at 1441 Secor Road until 1970, when he passed it onto his daughter, Elaine Schroeder Wright, who currently operates Myrtle Flowers at 5014 Dorr Street. *Submitted by Elaine Schroeder Wright, daughter of Allwin Schroeder.*

SHAVE AND A HAIRCUT.

Railroad detective turned barber, Ira Paul Raymond Meeks, stands before his shop circa 1926. Though the location is not certain, it is likely 229 Fearing Boulevard. It is positively identified as Meeks' by the name and initials on the window – I.P.R. Meeks. Mr. Meeks, a veteran of the Spanish-American War, made his home with wife, Marie (nee Gerver), in East Toledo. Their meeting according to family lore, "At one time he was a railroad detective and would wave at a young lady, along the right-of-way, by the name of Marie Gerver. One day he stopped the train and introduced himself and they later married." *Submitted by Lee Gagle.*

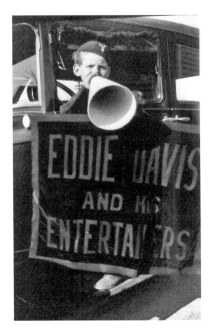

THE PITCHMAN.

A young Floyd C. Davis takes to the street in autumn, 1933, to create interest for dad's band, Eddie Davis and his Entertainers. *Submitted by Alan Davis, son of Floyd.*

SUNDAY IN THE PARK.

Lucille and Charles Payne enjoy a Sunday afternoon in Walbridge Park, overlooking the Maumee River, during the summer of 1923. *Submitted by Veronica Lawrence, daughter of Charles and Lucille Payne.*

COUNTER STAFF.

Six waitresses pose behind the lunch counter at downtown Toledo's F.W. Woolworth Five-and-Dime Store. Frank W. Woolworth was both pioneer and king of five-and-dime, chain-store- merchandising. He opened his first in Lancaster, Pennsylvania, in 1879. His aim was to offer low-cost items for frugal housewives. Toledo's popular Woolworth's was located at Adams and Superior streets. The large store also featured merchandise at the basement level. Kresge's, a major dime store competitor, was located just east in the same block at Adams and St. Clair streets. Earlier, McCrory's, another dime store chain, had an outlet at the corner of Summit Street and Madison Avenue. However, it was Woolworth's which outlasted all the competition downtown, including the major department stores, until it, too, closed in 1994. A new bank now occupies the beautifully renovated building. The ladies in this circa 1930 photograph are, from the left; Eva Weaver, Alberta Meyer, Evelyn Wallace, Mildred (last name unknown), Helen Wallace, and Mary Zalesak. *Submitted by Ron Kozina, nephew of Alberta Meyer.*

THE OTHER SIDE.

The United States Courthouse and Custom House was designed by Graham H. Woolfall to be the centerpiece of Toledo's planned Civic Center Mall. Now known simply as The Federal Courthouse, the building has identical elevations facing Ontario Street and Spielbusch Avenue. This photograph was probably taken from the Toledo Waterworks' building in the spring of 1932, from the Ontario Street side. The prominent roof line of the Hillcrest Hotel is seen on the horizon, to the left of the courthouse. The offices of the Blodgett-Beckley Company, coffee importers, are on Spielbusch Avenue, to the right. It wasn't until 1940 that the Civic Center Mall became a reality with the removal of this section of Ontario Street and a portion of Beech Street. The covered areas along Ontario Street may be stalls from the farmer's market that were later moved to the southeast corner of Orange Street and Spielbusch Avenue. *Submitted by Suzanne Dial. Caption written by Ken Dickson.*

YOUR CHAUFFEUR WAITS.

Edward E. Niemeyer, driver for the Community Traction Company, stretches his legs while on break from his Upton Avenue run in 1930. *Submitted by Margaret M. Hartford, Daughter of Edward E. Niemeyer.*

ROMANCE ON THE SHORE.
Louis Lewandowski romances his future wife Veronica Donnelly while overlooking Cullen Bay, summer, 1923. Louis' company, Lewandowski Engineering, was founded in 1916 and remains in business to this day. *Submitted by Ruth Lewandowski daughter-in-law of Louis and Veronica.*

EAST TOLEDO LANDMARK.
This 1930 photograph depicts the new Pennsylvania Railroad viaduct that crosses Main Street between Front Street and the Maumee River. The Cherry Street Bridge, which spans the river, is just behind the railroad viaduct. An incalculable number of vehicles have passed under this viaduct in the intervening years. *Submitted by and caption written by Ron Mauter.*

BEAUTY.

The classic lines of the art museum, beautiful landscaping, reflecting pond, and fountain provide the perfect setting for this summer photograph of Bessie Heinlen and her younger sister, Maxine. This circa 1915 view shows the Toledo Museum of Art just a few years after it opened on Monroe Street in 1912. Major additions, in 1926 and 1933, greatly expanded the museum to the size and appearance as we now know it. The landmark building with its park-like setting continue to provide a favored backdrop for special photography, especially wedding pictures. *Submitted by Carolyn Mavis. Caption written by Fred Folger.*

GLASS PLANT RAZING.

This Libbey Glass Manufacturing Company building is being neatly razed circa 1935. The building, at 1111 Buckeye Street, was part of Libbey's Westlake Division that developed and manufactured glass-making machinery. Libbey facilities remain on the larger site at Buckeye and Champlain streets, but all of these buildings and the railroad sidings have been removed. *Submitted by Virginia J. Wagoner.*

TYPE FACES.
Serious students, both male and female, concentrate on their typing skills in this 1925 Davis College class. Although the first electric typewriter was built by Thomas Alva Edison in the United States in 1872, the widespread use of electric typewriters was not common until the 1950s. *Submitted by Davis College.*

THE HAPPY COUPLE.
Love is in the air in the spring of 1930, as Fritz Melchior and his wife, Edna Liebnau Melchior, enjoy the sunshine. *Submitted by Jerry Melchior, son of Fritz and Edna Melchior.*

GALA OPENING.

It was February 16, 1929. The Paramount Theater marquee proclaims, "Gala Opening Today." People gather, with eager anticipation, on the Adams Street sidewalk to purchase tickets. Once inside the patrons were dazzled with the palace-like setting. Statues and plaster decoration had cost $400,000. Also, the theater, which seated 3,450 people, had a starlight ceiling with projected clouds. The Paramount has been described as a "Temple of the Cinema." People who remember seeing motion pictures or stage productions at the theater have special memories of those times. Notice the traffic and pedestrians at the Adams-Huron intersection. A Community Traction Co. bus stops at the corner by the popular Lasalle & Koch Department Store. The theater was razed in 1965 to make way for a parking lot. It was thirty-six years old at the time. *Submitted by the Toledo Area Regional Transit Authority (TARTA). Caption written by Fred Folger.*

I'M WITH THE BAND.
The Salvation Army band plays its way up Summit Street towards Jackson Street circa *1930. Submitted by Florence Stemen, band member.*

BREAD HOT.
The Pillsbury dough man has nothing over this cute young lady. Katherine Baker was turning heads on her Bond Bread delivery route on Huron Street in the mid-1930s. *Submitted by Florence Stemen.*

LOBBY ON A GRAND SCALE.
This grand lobby with its marble columns and skylight illumination was a memorable feature of Toledo's Secor Hotel. It was completed and opened in time to welcome many Union veterans of the Civil War in the summer of 1908. This was when Toledo hosted the annual G.A.R. (Grand Army of the Republic) encampment. Built of reinforced concrete and containing 400 rooms, the Secor was the city's leading hotel until 1927, when the Commodore Perry Hotel opened just across Superior Street. Many Toledoans have fond memories of the Secor's Candlelight Buffet in its later years. The hotel closed for business in 1969. *Submitted by Jerry Moore. Caption written by Fred Folger.*

111

HANGING WITH THE BOYS.

Four-year-old Florence Hamilton takes her turn on the tire swing in the backyard of her Ironville home on Jessie Street. Big brothers, Chuck on the right, and Edward Hamilton, wait their turn during the summer of 1932. *Submitted by Florence Hamilton Brown*

TO CLARENCE WITH LOVE.

The Keil family line the porch of their Belmar Avenue home to send a memento to a hospitalized Clarence Keil. From the left are: Benjamin Klute, James F. Keil, son of Clarence, Margaret Dargatz, Mary Ann Klute, Leona Keil, wife of Clarence, Amelia Keil, Katherine Welker, and John C. Keil, son of Clarence, and John J. Keil. *Submitted by Mark Keil, son of John C. Keil.*

FROSH FOOTBALLERS.

The 1931 edition of the Toledo University freshman football team is pictured here. The team was coached by Phil Moses. The third player from the left, in the center row is, Paul Wirick, Sr. Later, in 1948, Moses coached Paul Wirick, Jr. at Libbey High School. *Submitted by Paul Wirick, Jr., son of Paul Wirick, Sr.*

TELEGRAM PLACE.

Mrs. Fern Parish was operator of this Western Union office. The company's main office was in the Western Union Building at 523 Jefferson Street. There were a number of branch offices, most of which were downtown. Also shown in this August 15, 1931, photograph are, from the left, Stanley Adamski, Albert Yeager, Sr. and Brent Harris. Mr. Yeager also headed various activities at the Young Men's Christian Association (YMCA). *Submitted by Al Yeager, son of Albert Yeager.*

RIDING HIGH.

Three brave lads get the ride of a lifetime aboard Toots the Elephant at the Toledo Zoo circa 1932. *Submitted by Glen DeGelnor.*

TRADITIONAL.

Emil Herbac, Sr., and his daughter, Amelia, are dressed in traditional Czechoslovakian clothing. The photograph was taken at Sokol Moravan Hall on Valentine Street in East Toledo circa 1932. The garments were handmade in Emil's native country. Mr. Herbac met and married Catherine Jiskra, a fellow Czech, after immigrating to America. *Submitted by Emily Fluhrer, granddaughter of Emil Herbac, Sr. and niece of Amelia (Amy).*

OLD PAINT.

James R. Blum, President of The Dolphin Paint & Varnish Company stands by his 1934 DeSoto Air Flo. This photograph was taken outside his company's offices at 922 Locust Street, corner of Champlain Street circa 1934. Dolphin began in Toledo in 1885 as The Dolphin White Lead & Color Works at 28 Summit Street. After a fire and subsequent move, the enterprise located at 922 Locust circa 1921. Mr. Blum joined the company in 1918. He became President in 1933 and held that position until he retired in 1945. The Dolphin Company is still in operation at the Locust Street address. *Submitted by James Blum, grandson of James R. Blum.*

NEXT STOP – BAY SHORE ROAD.

Mrs. Virginia Binkley Wiezbicki, pictured here in the early 1920s, was one of a handful of female bus drivers in the country. Working for her brother, Joseph Gates, owner of Harbor View Transit Lines, Mrs. Binkley began her 20-year bus driving career in 1921. Harbor View Transit Lines started from the Gates home on Bay Shore Road with a horse and buggy and a single route to Ironville. The company later added busses and extended service to Genoa, Curtice, Williston and Clay Center. *Submitted by Suzanne St. John, granddaughter of Virginia Binkley Wiezbicki.*

1933 Thomas A. DeVilbiss High School Football Team

Athletic Director
Norman Pollman

Football Coach
Harry Rice

FIRST TIGER ELEVEN.

After two preliminary seasons, the Thomas A. DeVilbiss High School fielded its first varsity football team in the fall of 1933. The Tigers, wearing orange and black, won their first victory five games into the season against Adrian, and in the season's last game won their first of what would be many Toledo City League victories. In that game, won 7-0 against Woodward, this photograph's donor, Bill Wyatt, caught a pass for the DeVilbiss extra point. Wyatt is in the top row, third man from the left and may be the only surviving member of this team. Prominent in the photograph are Athletic Director Norman Pollman, on the left, and Football Coach Harry Rice. *Submitted by Bill Wyatt.*

PONY UP.
Six year old Fred Hepner poses on a pony in front of his home at 952 Colburn Street in June of 1936. Enterprising photographers of the day would outfit a child, place him on the pony, and then ring the doorbell for the unsuspecting parent. At least in Fred's case, the parent could not resist and purchased this photograph from the roaming photographer. *Submitted by Fred Hepner.*

SISTERS AND BROTHER.
Three of the seventeen siblings of the community-conscious Gonzalez family pose in 1935. Alice Gonzalez is holding her baby sister, Maria Sue Gonzalez, while their brother, Francisco Gonzalez, stands by them. Each sibling worked for the betterment of the Hispanic community of Northwestern Ohio. Alice is an Ursuline nun, Sister Maria Jose, Frank was a volunteer translator for the courts, and Maria Sue Campos is an advocate of Hispanic rights. *Submitted by Salud Gonzalez De Cortez, sister of all.*

BUSMAN'S HOLIDAY.

Louis H. Banks was a landscape gardener by profession. Here, he tends to the grounds at his own home circa 1925. Mr. Banks and his wife, Margaret, lived at 628 Pinewood Avenue. *Submitted by Calvin Banks, Sr., grandson of Louis H. Banks.*

PRESS RUN.

Wilbur J. Fern, Pressroom Foreman for the Toledo News-Bee, checks his work on the April 27, 1938 edition. The News-Bee was a Scripps-Howard Newspaper that published daily in Toledo for many years, but ceased in August, 1938. The company's operations were downtown at Huron and Jackson streets. Mr. Fern had previously been a pressman for The Toledo Blade. After the News-Bee closed, he returned to The Blade. *Submitted by Richard Fern, son of Wilbur J. Fern.*

HOT DOG!

The staff of Toledo Hot Dog lines up behind the counter for this circa 1937 photograph. The downtown eatery began serving meals at this 449 St. Clair Street at Jackson Street location in 1937. Customers were often those patronizing the nearby theaters and entertainment district. Head cook, Nick Nicolaidis, is the second man from the left. *Submitted by Elaine Nicolaidis, daughter of Nick Nicolaidis.*

DRESSED FROM HEAD TO TOE.

A dapper Maurice "Bernie" Feder stands outside of The Franklin Bargain House on East Woodruff Street during the spring of 1935. The men's store was owned by Bernie's father-in-law Louis Ellison. *Submitted by Marcia Feder-Knorek, daughter of Bernie Feder and Lena Ellison Feder.*

COMPANY PICNIC.

These men are the machine repairmen and mill-wrights of Building 15 at the Auto-Lite plant. The drink of choice appears to be beer at this picnic gathering in October, 1935. Harold Liggett is standing directly in front of the window. *Submitted by Richard Ingalsbe, son-in-law of Harold Liggett.*

MONKEYING AROUND AT THE MONKEY HOUSE.

Gordon, Rendal, Shirley, Donna, and Jim Holder patiently pose for this photo in 1936 in front of the monkey house at the Toledo Zoo. Clearly, little Jim would rather be monkeying around than posing for a photo. *Submitted by Shirley Holder Montague.*

ALL WET.

Maynard "Joe" Curtis, civil engineer for the City of Toledo, surveys flooded Jackman Road near Woodlawn Cemetery circa 1937. *Submitted by Martha Curtis Ball, daughter of Maynard Curtis.*

HERE'S TO YOU.

Ignatius Coehrs, with a full glass, is relaxing with his friends after a hard day's work circa 1935. They seem to be enjoying their Happy Hour. *Submitted by Amy Sanislo, great-grandniece of Ignatius Coehrs.*

LET'S ALL GO DOWN TO TIEDTKES.

Eleanor Pietrykowski worked for Tiedtke's for over 25 years, but is not identified in this circa 1935 photograph of the store. Mr. Sochaki is in the front row, on the left, and the two young girls in the front center are Mary Jane Sochaki and Gertrude Sochaki. *Submitted by Christine Pietrykowski, daughter-in-law of Eleanor Pietrykowski.*

CRISP & DELICIOUS.

The Manhattan Potato Chip Company fleet assembled at the company's head-quarters at 2423 Lagrange Street in 1935. Checking a can of chips is the company's bookkeeper, Joseph D. Jankowski (white shirt). Leo J. Jankowski was president of the enterprise which was incorporated in 1929. Next door is Andrew Pytel's restaurant and home at 3425 Lagrange Street. *Submitted by James M. Weislak, nephew of Joseph D. Jankowski.*

TOLEDO BREW.

Buckeye Beer began brewing in Toledo in 1872 and outlasted all of its many 19th century competitors. Buckeye became a staple among Toledo beer drinkers and was brewed locally until 1972. This photograph depicts one of the company's delivery trucks, decked out, probably for a parade circa 1935, Buckeye's heyday. *Submitted by Sharon Yaros.*

A WHOLE NEW WORLD.

Young Donald Brown stands on the front porch of his home at 207 East Woodruff Street. The neighborhood has changed a great deal since this 1938 photo. Only the building at the end of the street remains. *Submitted by Donald Brown.*

121

MAN IN BLUE.

William Clemens Benner is shown as a "rookie" member of the Toledo Police Department in 1914 and later in his service with a partner. The second picture was taken in 1935 at the police sub-station that operated out of the Toledo Fire Department, Station Number 18 located at Sylvania Avenue and Peak Street. This station is now the home of the Toledo Firefighters Museum. *Submitted by Mary Lou Pifer, daughter of William Clemens Benner.*

"ROTH MOTOR SALES — NOV. 10, 1936"

THE MECHANICS.

Members of The Roth Motor Sales Company service department pose at their workplace at 1306-1312 Cherry Street on November 10, 1936. The Roth new-car dealership was incorporated in 1926 by Roscoe H. Roth. Later, he was joined by his brother Leland C. Roth in management of the firm. They described their enterprise as "Dealers in Pontiac Motor Cars and Nearly New Used Cars." The dealership moved several times over the years, always to a Cherry Street address, before shutting down its new car sales division in 1981. At that time, Roth was headed by Gene Roth, the founder's son, who continued in used car sales. Many Toledoans recall being greeted at the final location, 1721 Cherry Street, by a statue of a formally-dressed Native American, with arm upraised. *Submitted by Carolyn Owens.*

Grace E. Smith

TIME TO EAT!

Toledo restaurateur extraordinaire Grace E. Smith, opened Smith's Cafeteria at Madison Avenue and Erie Street in a busy downtown Toledo in June of 1936, the year of this photograph. In addition to the cafeteria, Smith's business also featured a coffee shop, a service dining room, and a pastry shop. Within two years the cafeteria was serving more than 1,000,000 meals annually and quickly became a Toledo institution that employed nearly 200 people at its peak. The downtown facility closed in the early 1970s. Miss Smith operated a number of Toledo restaurants, but Smith's Cafeteria is her legacy. She also became the first female President of the National Restaurant Association. *Submitted by Sandra Smith Reams, grand-niece of Grace E. Smith.*

OH MY ACHING BACK.

These men are cleaning the floor of a gallery at The Toledo Museum of Art during September, 1937. Bill Salisbury is in the rear. *Submitted by Jerry Flahie.*

RAILROAD TIES GALORE!

Railroad ties were treated with creosote at this Jennison-Wright Company facility at 2463 Broadway in Toledo. This photograph of the Yard Group was taken on April 29, 1937. Most of the men pictured here were employed to carry the ties through the process at the 26-acre site. Pay was on a piecework basis and the work was extremely heavy (note the protective leather shoulder pads). Crossties were eight feet in length and weighed up to 200 pounds while switch ties, or sluggers, were even larger. Three cents was earned for each of the crossties carried while four to five cents was paid for each slugger. Samuel Hunt, near the top of the picture and holding his shoulder strap, provided the details of the operation. *Submitted by Beverly Beasley and Dwayne Todd Archie, and caption written by Dwayne Todd Archie.*

1. Stanley Thurman, 2. Eddie Harris, 3. John Miller, General Foreman, 4. P. O'Neal,
5. Hank Wolfe, Yard Foreman, 6. Grant Davis, 7. Milton, 8. Elijah Campbell, 9. Townsville Harris,
10. Jones, 11. Samuel Hunt, 12. the owner's son, 13. Otis Wakefield, 14. Johnny Johnson,
15. Raymond Cooksie, 16. Ulysses Harris, 17. Ambrose Scott, 18. Jesse Bruce,
19. Hobart Morris, 20. Mr. Kelly, 21. Otis Cooksie, 22. George Inman, 23. Mr. Gilbert,
24. Gather Thorpe, 25. Clarence Johnson, 26. Mr. Smith, 27. Augustus Hamilton,
28. and 29 unidentified checkers, 30 and 31 unknown.

SHOE REPAIR.

Paul George operated this large shoe repair shop at 314 Superior Street, in downtown Toledo, as well as another in the 1600 block of Broadway. In 1937 his shops were among more than 150 operating in the city. Today, there are less than ten, two of which are operated by Mr. George's great-grandnephews, Daniel and Dimitri Georgevich. *Submitted by Deena Georgevich Brueshaber, great-grandniece of Paul George.*

FT. MEIGS IN WINTER.

Florence and Dell Barhite do not let a little snow stop their visit to Fort Meigs during the winter of 1939. *Submitted by Christine Martin, granddaughter of Florence and Dell Barhite.*

DOOOOWWWWWNNTOWN

Winter, 1937, finds Roth Furs right where you would expect them to be....Downtown. The Bell & Beckwith brokerage house is next door, to the left. *Submitted by Phillip Roth.*

125

LUTHERANS ON COURTHOUSE SQUARE.

These young Lutherans are delegates to the seventh annual convention of the Michigan District Luther League held in October of 1937 at St. Paul's Lutheran Church in downtown Toledo. The congregation has occupied this Erie Street location, between Adams and Jackson, since the "Wooden Church" (inset) was built in 1858. The present structure, shown here, was dedicated in 1868. Major renovations, interior and exterior, were completed in 1953, giving the church, facing the Lucas County Courthouse, its present look. *Submitted by St. Paul's Historian James R. Blum and Ann Wajer.*

FAMILY BAKERY.

The Lutz Bakery Company staff lined up for this photograph on March 18, 1937. Lutz was a wholesale baker located at 201 Sylvania Avenue. The company's officers were all named Lutz. Jacob was President, John was Vice-President, and Harry was Secretary-Treasurer. Harry Young is in the top row, fourth from the left. His wife, Margaret, is fourth from the left in the middle row. The couple had met while working at Lutz and married in 1935. *Submitted by Carol Queenan, daughter of Harry and Margaret Young.*

GROCERY FLOATING DELIVERY

The Edgewater Market, located at 5202 Summit Street in Point Place, operated this supply boat that serviced ships docking at the Port of Toledo. In this photograph from about 1938, Steve Werkman, Jr. looks back at the freighter CLETUS SCHNEIDER, after delivering groceries and meats to her cook. Orders were phoned to the store early in the day. *Submitted by Stephen Werkman.*

SERVICE WITH A SMILE.

Clarence Sauer, second from the left in the second row, and his fellow service men of the Sears Super Station on Summit Street, near Monroe Street take a moment for this photograph before the start of business on April 27, 1937. *Submitted by Bonna Weaver, daughter of Clarence Sauer.*

HEAVY DUTY.

The crew at the Toledo Machine and Tool Company, Plant 2, paused long enough for this photograph on March 3, 1937. The foundry operation was at 1420 Hastings Avenue at Dorr Street. Frank J. Swy, in the front row, is smoking his pipe. *Submitted by Al Yeager, grandson of Frank J. Swy.*

WHAT A WOMAN.

The Mumma Plumbing and Heating girls softball team was among the best in Toledo in 1937. One of the reasons for the team's success was the strong play of Sylvia Yourist, the first player from the left in the back row. Miss Yourist was an outstanding all-around athlete, and was also Captain of the Kewpee Hamburg girls basketball team. She played girls football as well, and was a participant in, what was billed as the, "First Girls Football Game Played Under Collegiate Rules." She played right tackle for the East Side against a West Side team. The milestone game was played Sunday, December 3, 1933 at Swayne Field. *Submitted by Daryl Yourist, nephew of Sylvia Yourist.*

FIRST CLASS.

Too new for uniforms, the first Toledo Police Academy Class stands proudly at the pistol range in 1938. Donald Larson, fourth from the left, back row, went on to a 26-year career with the Toledo Police Department. *Submitted by Nelle Larson, wife of Donald Larson.*

POLO PRIZE.

Ruth Dodge presents a championship trophy to three gentlemen still attired in their distinctive and protective polo gear at the Carranor Hunt and Polo Club in Perrysburg. The trophy was the Carranor Cup and the year was about 1938. Accepting is Rathbun Fuller Mather, as Bower Corwin looks on. Rathbun Fuller Mather was the son of Gordon McDonald Mather, founder of the Mather Spring Company. The identity of the gentleman on the far right is not known. *Submitted by Christine Mather Bothe, daughter of Rathbun Fuller Mather.*

CLASSIC LOBBY.

The beautiful lobby of the Paramount Theatre (see page 110) is shown here in the fall of 1937. The display items promote a drawing for a new 1938 Chrysler Royal. The automobile was offered by the Reilly-Wearley Company (Chrysler distributors) and chances were obtained with a purchase at Bellman Super Markets. *Submitted by Marie Wenzlick.*

ONE RINGY-DINGY. TWO RINGY-DINGYS.

Telephone operator, Alocia Hoffman, is working at an Ohio Bell branch office switchboard in 1939. This equipment was located at 116 Hall Street, Holland, Ohio, in the residence of Zelda and Vincent Schwind. This type of switchboard was used with crank telephones. *Submitted by Vivian M. Snyder, daughter of Zelda M. Schwind.*

129

PAPER GIRL.

Four-year-old Mary Katherine Kuesthardt peeks out the window of this Commerce Paper Company truck in 1939. Her father, Edgar Leslie Kuesthard, was one of three partners who founded the Toledo business in 1931. Edgar and his two partners, Walter Riopelle and Orville Woods, first located their business in a leased multi-story building at 38 North St. Clair Street near Monroe Street, perhaps the setting for this photograph. Mary is now Mrs. S. Dean Roberts. Her husband was President of The Commerce Paper Company from 1964 through 1995. Now, her son, Craig D, Roberts, heads the company. *Submitted by Craig D. Roberts, son of Mary Katherine Kuesthardt Roberts.*

TRAVELLING ICE.

These men are loading ice from People's Ice and Coal Company into a refrigerator car of the Great Northern Railroad circa 1938. *Submitted by Edna and Donald R. Burwell, Sr.*

LONG TIME GROCER.

Howard N. Warner, third from the left, poses with the staff of his grocery store at 305 Dixie Highway circa 1939. Warner was a long-time (see page 79) Rossford grocer, operating a Dixie Highway store for 30 years before he retired. *Submitted by Nancy Stonerock, granddaughter of Howard N. Warner.*

CANDID CAMERA.

A roving photographer caught William A. Fox walking down Adams Street, east of Superior Street. The legendary Paramount Theater is in the background. *Submitted by Bobbi Beagle, daughter of William A. Fox.*

ROYAL CROWN.

Helen and Al Duke opened the Crown Market on the corner of Walnut and Bancroft streets in the mid 1940s. Helen's sister Marcie Toth Bronowski, continues to operate the store. *Submitted by Iris Trzcinski, niece of Helen and Marcie.*

"WIN WITH WILLKIE"

was the Republican slogan in the 1940 presidential campaign. Here, we see the Willkie Clubs headquarters in the Colton Building, located on Madison Avenue at Erie Street. A truck with a large Willkie broadside is parked at the curb. The 1940 campaign was unique. The incumbent, Franklin D. Roosevelt, was seeking an unprecedented third term. His Republican challenger, Wendell Willkie was a former Democrat, a Wall Street lawyer, and utilities executive. He had no political experience. He entered no primaries, made no deals, and organized no campaign. He was enthusiastic and articulate. His energy inspired followers to circulate petitions and sponsor Willkie appearances. By the time of the party convention, the chant, "We Want Willkie," was predominant. He was nominated on the sixth ballot to the dismay of the Republican Old Guard. World War II overshadowed the election. On November 5, President Roosevelt won his third term, carrying thirty-eight states to Willkie's ten states. Among the onlookers, Arnold Bunge, Sr. is the third from the right. *Submitted by Rick Bunge, grandson of Arnold Bunge, Sr. Caption written by Fred Folger.*

FLOWER HOSPITAL.

Miss Gertrude Sheriff, with an armful of books, stands facing Cherry School. She taught the fourth grade there when this photograph was taken in May, 1940. Behind her, on the west side of Cherry Street, near Collingwood Boulevard is the first Flower Hospital. *Submitted by Winifred McBeth.*

POLICE BADGE NUMBER ONE.

Patrolman Andrew Iwinski, known as Andy to the countless Toledoans who knew him, directs traffic at the corner of Summit and Monroe streets. He spent nearly 46 years as a Toledo Police Officer and earned the distinction of wearing the Department's number one badge as its senior member. Officer Iwinski directed traffic with a semaphore until traffic lights took over that job. *Submitted by Evelyn Nowak, daughter of Andrew Iwinski.*

BETTER THAN LIVE TELEVISION.

Ruth Goldie Hipkiss makes a beautiful model in the window of the S.S. Kresge store. She is introducing the new, fashionable silk stockings to the Toledo market circa 1940. *Submitted by Dorothy Johansen, niece of Armon Van Natta, Ruth Goldie Hipkiss' husband.*

DOUBLE DUTY.

Members of The American Legion Police Post #512 march east on Jefferson Street, just past Erie Street in 1940. The men of this unit are all veterans who served during wartime and are also Toledo Police Officers. They are led here by the post's first Vice-Commander, Charles Dolley. Post #512 was chartered in the summer of 1939. *Submitted by Tammy Wheeler, daughter of Charles Dolley.*

ON A ROLL.

Carmen Williamson snapped this shot of his buddies shooting dice in an alley behind Goodman's Bakery in the summer of 1941. Left to right are: Marshall Dunn, Bob Donald-El, Grover Donald-El, Bud White, Walter Segail, Jr., on the fence, Edward Crow, and an unknown man. The alley was between Scott Street and Woodruff Avenue. *Submitted by Carmen Williamson.*

SAVE ME SOME.

Big brother Robert Krieger, Jr. does not seem interested in sharing his drink with his little sister, Carol Ann. Bob and Carol lived at 835 Vinton Street. It appears that this was a hot day when the photograph was taken in 1941. *Submitted by Robert Krieger, Jr.*

133

FIFTEEN MINUTES OF FAME.

Representatives, from the bakers of Wonder Bread, featured grocer Roman S. Zawodni in this 1940 advertisement for their product. Roman and his father, Frank, operated Zawodni's Market on Avondale Avenue at Hoag Street. *Submitted by Roman H. Zawodni, son of Roman S. Zawodni.*

GARAGE RAISING.

From the left, Arthur Jones, Luelva May Jones, Marie Benner, and her husband, Vern, pose while getting together at the Jones' farm. Vern is helping his father-in-law build a garage at 9435 Sylvania Avenue in Sylvania. This photograph is from 1941. *Submitted by Marjorie Achinger, daughter of Marie and Vern Benner.*

THE GANG'S ALL HERE.

Lined up and ready to ride on May 9, 1946, are, from the left; Pete Berkabile, Toby Ward, Fritz Ward, Paula Deatrick, Carolyn Nagle, and Jeff Kilmer, all of Island Avenue. Carolyn seems to be missing a bicycle. *Submitted by Paula Deatrick Ashton.*

DUAL CELEBRATION.

Stephen and his sister, Dolores Binkowski, celebrate their First Communion, May, 1941. Gathered, from the left are: Ron Gniewkowski, Helen Binkowski, Stella Gniewkowski, Ed Binkowski, Mary Binkowski and Stella Binkowski. *Submitted by Stephen Binkowski.*

FLYING HIGH.

Anthony Fabiszak took this great shot of his boys February 12, 1941 at Toledo Municipal Airport. Richard, six, on the left, and Thomas, four, were able to see the planes close-up. *Submitted by Ann Fabiszak Payne, sister of Richard and Thomas.*

CAN CAN.

Office and plant employees of The American Can Company, tinware manufacturers, are neatly organized for this August, 1941, photograph. Walter Witaszek, wearing suspenders, is in the third row. The plant was at City Park Avenue and Hamilton Street. The sign describes the function of this group as, "Paint & Spray Department 1. Toledo Factory 59A." *Submitted by Nancy Vuketich, niece of Walter Witaszek.*

WRECKED.
Jerry Throne was not happy to see his new 1941 tow truck smashed by a drunk driver. Fortunately, the crash occurred directly in front of his auto repair shop on Upton Avenue. Throne's continue their towing and repair work at the same location today. *Submitted by Jerry Throne.*

PUTTIN' ON THE RITZ.
George and Margaret Gurcsik, operators of Oregon's long-time restaurant, The Ritz Supper Club, stand at the eatery's entrance circa 1942. George's parent's, Steve and Rose Gurcsik, were Hungarian immigrants who began the business in 1937. Margaret continued to operate the restaurant until it closed in 1989. *Submitted by Lori Gurcsik Bolone, granddaughter of George and Margaret Gurcsik.*

TODDLING.
Carol Ardner, one and a half years old, walks up her grandmother's driveway at 907 Superior Street (see page 82) during the winter of 1943-1944. The former Westminster Presbyterian Church is in the background. *Submitted by Carol Ardner.*

SCHOOL'S OUT.
Thomas Jacobs, third from the left in the third row from the top, looks proud, as do his 44 classmates, to be graduating from St. Mary's School on Cherry Street. Father Boucher is seated in the front. The graduation picture was taken June, 1943. *Submitted by Bonnie Peer, daughter of Thomas Jacobs.*

NIGHT ON THE TOWN.

In 1943, Ka-See's Nite Club on Lagrange Street was the place to be. Madeline Larberg, on the far right, enjoys a night of music and dancing with her friends. From the left they are: Elaine Higgins, Arlene Thomas, and Betty Paxton. Submitted by Madeline Larberg Drozdowicz.

FAMILY REUNION.

Three brothers (numbered from the left), Aloysious Sobczak (1), Edward Sobczak (4), and Leonard Sobczak (5), are joined by their cousins, Eugene Simmons (2) and Ray Szymanowski (3), for a Toledo reunion in 1943. *Submitted by Patricia Presser, niece of the Sobczak brothers.*

SPOTLESS.

A neatly-uniformed June Mehlow, polishes the windshield of her sparkling clean Red Cab in autumn, 1943. The Red Cab Company facilities were located at 213-227 14th Street across from the main Post Office which is seen in the background of this photograph. The Red Cab Company actually operated two taxicab services, Red and Yellow, both accessed by the easily remembered phone number, MAin 1-2-3-4. President of the company was Frank Lockhard, a former star quarterback at the University of Notre Dame. The Red Cab Company property was sold to the adjacent Toledo Club in 1961 and is now used for parking. *Submitted by Cynthia Mehlow Machnicki, granddaughter of June Mehlow.*

A SIGN OF THE TIMES.

The subjects of this photograph, women and children, were not unusual ones during World War II. The fathers of these two young boys, Charles Miller, on the left, and John Husman, were overseas as a part of the war effort. Dorothy Chapman, on the far left, holds her grandson Charles while her mother, Mary Richmond, holds John. Dorothy's daughters, Jeanne Miller, on the left, and Ruth Husman are the mothers of the boys. This early 1943 photograph, depicting four generations, was taken at Dorothy's home on West Grove Place. *Submitted by Michelle H. Marciniak, daughter of John Husman.*

BUS DRIVER

Bowdoin Exeter Davis worked for The Community Traction Company for 49 years. This snapshot of Mr. Davis in his uniform was taken downtown in 1944. Drivers were required to make change for fares, hence the coin changer attached to his belt. *Submitted by Jeanne Belding, daughter of Bowdoin Exeter Davis.*

TRUCK DRIVER.

Delbert Barhite was a truck driver for over 30 years. Pictured here in the fall of 1942 are Mr. Barhite, on the far left, and other unknown gentlemen outside The National Transit Corporation warehouse at 660 Sterling Street. *Submitted by Delbert R. Barhite, son of Delbert A. Barhite.*

EYES ON THE PRIZE.

Helen Hampton, fourth from the left, has her eyes set on Jim Campbell, her date for the Waite High School Senior Prom January, 1945. To the couple's right are: Clayton Scott, Joy Hardy, Bill Gregus, Helen's sister, Donna Hampton, Bob Nomar, and Janet Blossom. The identity of the couple on the left is not known. *Submitted by Helen Hampton Campbell, blissfully married to Jim Campbell since January, 1950.*

SWEPT AWAY.

Jean Duda is happy to see her fiancé, Joseph Cieslukowski, home on leave from the The Merchant Marine in the spring of 1945. The couple married later that year. *Submitted by Annie Cieslukowski, daughter of Joseph and Jean Cieslukowski.*

THANK YOU FOR SHOPPING AT KROGER.

Twyla Sebring (in glasses), grocery manager, and Dorothy Whiteman, clerk, wait on shoppers at the Kroger store located at 1315 Detroit Avenue near Dorr Street. Meat manager, Adolph Kalmbach (in the white hat) and unknown customers look on in November, 1944. *Submitted by Becky Sebring-Huerta, daughter of Twyla Sebring.*

139

NO SELF SERVE.

With the full service stations of 1949, Joe Kovesdi didn't need to get out of his 1936 Ford to pump his own gasoline. This photograph was taken at the Hi-Speed filling station at Front and Consaul streets. Mr. Kovesdi lived at 2613 York Street. *Submitted by Joseph and Dorothy Kovesdi.*

MA AND PA GRZECHOWIAK.

Stephen and Rose Grzechowiak, of Marmion Street, couldn't look happier if they tried. *Submitted by Christine Grzechowiak, wife of Robert Grzechowiak, whose grandparents are pictured.*

JAUNTY GENTS.

Two dapper gentlemen, Cleveland Williams in the hat, and Albert Ellis, are ready to step out. The picture was taken circa 1940s. *Submitted by Marnette L. Cunningham, granddaughter of Cleveland Williams.*

HAT'S & TIES & MORE.

Jack's Men's Shop was founded by a father and son team in 1929. Jack Steinman and his son Alvin, shown in the photograph above, observed the motto, "We always have the latest styles first." That philosophy served them well, as Alvin continued to operate the store until he retired in 1976. The outside of the store, at 419 Summit Street, is shown to the right in 1948. Jack's Men's Wear is still in operation today at 3402 Dorr Street. *Submitted by Julie Ellison, granddaughter of Alvin Steinman and great-granddaughter of Jack Steinman.*

SHOPPING ON SUMMIT.

Woodward High School sophomore, Daisy Gable, stopped to pose while shopping on Summit Street in the autumn of 1945. *Submitted by Daisy Gable Moore.*

141

BIKING IN IRONVILLE.

Brothers, James (left) and Charles Crowder, pose at Henry Tiedjen's filling station in 1946. The Tiedjen Sohio station, on the northeast corner of Clarence and Front streets, was the only gasoline outlet in the Ironville neighborhood. Henry Tiedjen made his home just a few doors away at 3020 Front Street. The Crowder boys and their parents, Tolbert and Cloie Crowder, lived at 386 Millard (at the corner of Tiffin Avenue). The boys attended Irving School. Seen in the background, through the building windows, is the Unitcast Steel Foundry. *Submitted by Mike Crowder, son of Charles Crowder.*

FIVE GUYS IN A TRUNK.

In the fall of 1945, George Thabit, second from the left, and his buddies are doing what they do the best, hanging out and having fun around Erie and Chestnut streets. Stuffed in the trunk are, from the left, Donald Francis, George Thabit, James Sahadi, Francis Kirdahy, and Joe Gunzleman. *Submitted by George Thabit.*

BUZZ CUT MISS?

Fred Kirdahy, the barber on the left, was a master with a straight razor and clippers for more than 50 years. Here he cuts for a lady at his 714 Cherry Street shop circa 1945. *Submitted by Tony Kirdahy, nephew of Fred Kirdahy.*

LABOR ON PARADE.

This parade, moving east on Monroe Street and curving to the north on Summit Street circa 1946, shows marchers wearing shirts reading Auto-Lite, while others carry Local 12 banners. Businesses on the south

side of Monroe Street extending from Summit are Behan's filling station, the Spangler Candy Company, Rogers Cigar Store, and Liberal Loan Pawnbrokers. The large building on the corner of the intersecting street is the Commerce Paper Company which faces St. Clair Street. The light-colored, three-story building on the opposite corner of St. Clair is Weber's Clothing House, the present site of Fifth Third Field. *Submitted by Mike Marciniak.*

RIZZO BROTHERS HOME FROM WAR.

Brothers, (from the left), Angelo, John, Dominic, and Felix Rizzo are being honored at a dinner and ceremony at the Commodore Perry Hotel in 1946 for World War II Italian-American servicemen. *Submitted by Ann Marie Rizzo Banas, daughter of John Rizzo.*

STRETCH YOUR SHOES?

Every imaginable shoe service was available at this Kennedy Shoe Repair shop located downtown in Tiedtke's Department Store, as viewed in this 1940 photograph. Joseph Miracola, middle shoemaker, was born in Massini, Italy, came to America in 1902, and, after a stay in Cleveland, came to Toledo in 1920. A shoemaker all his life, he reared a family of five and retired in 1952. He died in 1965. *Submitted by Ginny Smith, granddaughter of Joseph Miracola.*

THE ANDERSONS
SERVICE, GROWTH & CHANGE SINCE 1947

Harold Anderson was a dreamer and risk taker who understood the grain business and knew he could serve the farmer better.

In his wildest dreams he could not have imagined that the 500,000 bushel Maumee elevator terminal he and his sons built in 1946 would evolve into one of the largest grain operations in North America. Another "silo raising" in 1950 and the nationally publicized "Big Pour" in 1953 quadrupled the company's grain storage capacity. A cob milling plant opened in 1958, followed by a fertilizer blending operation, 22 more steel storage tanks and a deep-water river elevator in 1959. Today, the Agriculture Group operates grain elevators, fertilizer distribution terminals and farm centers in 4 states. Together they handle in excess of 150 million bushels of grain and 1.2 million tons of fertilizer products annually.

Harold's innovative plans led the company to diversify into a number of related businesses. The Warehouse Market opened in 1952, selling farm supplies to customers for their backhaul. The Retail Group now operates six stores in Ohio, offering a unique "More For Your Home®" blend of products and services from windows to wines.

In 1963, the company opened one of the most efficient fertilizer mixing plants ever conceived, producing fertilizer, insecticides and herbicides in a variety of lawn care products. The Processing Group currently provides fertilizer products for golf courses, lawn care operators and retailers across the country. A corncob milling plant was added in 1958, thereby turning a negative, corncob disposal, into yet another positive business venture. Today, The Andersons corncob-based products are used in a multitude of applications, from animal bedding to ice melters.

After a half-century of managing, maintaining and repairing its own fleet of railcars, The Andersons opened a Railcar Repair Shop in the 1990s. Fleet management services to private railcar owners, along with custom steel fabrication are now available. The company's current fleet of almost 18,800 railcars and 114 locomotives makes it one of the ten largest rail leasing companies in North America. Building on strengths and taking advantage of opportunities; that's what Harold Anderson had in mind almost sixty years ago, and why **The Andersons Mission Statement** remains as true today as it did when he founded the company in 1947.

We firmly believe that our company is a powerful vehicle through which we channel our time, talent, and energy in pursuit of the fundamental goal of serving God by serving others. Through our collective action we greatly magnify the impact of our individual efforts to:
- Provide extraordinary service to our customers
- Help each other improve • Support our communities
- Increase the value of our company

The Andersons

THE O'CONNELL LINE.

Meet the fierce linemen of the Toledo Mercurys hockey team. Lead by Barney O'Connell, in the middle, Jake Kernahan, on the right, and Orville Smith on the left. The O'Connell line ruled the ice in 1947. *Submitted by Tim O'Connell, son of Barney O'Connell.*

THE CLUBHOUSE.

John "Louis" Molnar took this snapshot of, from the left, Emery Hornyak, Eddie Bires, and John Szanto in front of their garages-converted-to-clubhouse on Valentine Street during the winter of 1947. The resourceful lads built their own ping pong table. *Submitted by Joseph "Louis" Molnar.*

GOING FOR A SPIN.

Mrs. Steinmiller goes for a spin on Linmore Street in 1946. She is sitting next to her son, Bob, who is behind the wheel. Her daughter, Virginia, rides in the back (left) with her friend Marilyn Schoof. *Submitted by William Schoof, Jr.*

PARTY TIME.

The kids are ready for birthday cake. This 1946 party at Christine and Harry Szmania's Mettler Street home includes party goers, from the left: Jack Rutkowski, an unidentified family friend, Patsy Woods, Tommy Szmania, Donnie Olzak, Rosann Szmania, Eileen Czerniak, and standing John Czerniak, holding Bobby Woods. *Submitted by Bob and Karen Woods. Bob is a grandson of John Czerniak.*

ONE OF A KIND IN TOLEDO

Harold and Shirley Jaffe pose with their son, Jeff, in front of Harold's Jewelry, on Cherry Street circa 1947. As the business grew, the Jaffe's eventually moved the store to Lewis Avenue in Temperance in 1950, then Dundee Street in Petersburg from 1952-1955, and subsequently, the Country Charm Shopping Center in Perrysburg from 1955-1965. They then moved to 3330 Secor Road in Toledo, calling the store Harold Jaffe Jewelers, staying there from 1964-1974. In 1974, the store moved into the Westgate Shopping Center and remained there until 1984. Harold Jaffe Jewelers then moved to the free standing store at 5055 Monroe Street and stayed there until June, 2004, when the store moved to its present Talmadge Road location. "Dad always said that he was on a ten year plan which was what happened with the Perrysburg, the Secor Road, and the Westgate Stores...Monroe became a twenty year plan," explained Jeff. As the business expanded, so did the Jaffe family. Bruce was born in 1950 and Ivan arrived in 1958. *Submitted by Jeff Jaffe*

HAPPY STUFFING.

This happy group of ladies, and one gentleman, is obviously having fun making kielbasa in November, 1948. From the left are; Connie Slowinski, Cecilia Bas Slowinski, Mrs. Klofta, Joseph Slowinski, and Mrs. Dymbowski. *Submitted by Danita Binkowski, niece of Connie Slowinski and granddaughter of Joseph and Cecilia Slowinski.*

FOOT BATH.

Carol Husen, three years old, cools her tootsies in a petunia-circled fountain at the old waterworks (now Danny Thomas Park), on Broadway in 1948. *Submitted by Carolyn Husen.*

NEW WHEELS.

A very happy Diane Widmer, white gloves and all, wheeled her new tricycle over to her Grandmother Bertha Waldvogel's, home in the 1800 block of Wyndhurst Road on April 11, 1948. *Submitted by Diane Widmer Zenk.*

PREPARING FOR WINTER.

It is warm weather, but Joseph Slowinski, of 1121 Woodstock, is filling the coal bin for the coming winter in June, 1948. *Submitted by Mary Ann Binkowski, daughter of Joseph Slowinski.*

FAMOUS GRADUATE.

Edith Johns is seated, second from the left, among her classmates of the Lagrange School Class of 1948. Also in the class, is Jameel Joseph Farah. Jameel, third from the right in the middle row, is now known as Jamie Farr. *Submitted by Doris Johns, sister-in-law of Edith Johns.*

147

FUTURE EDUCATORS.

In 1934, who would have dreamed Edrene and James Benson would both grow up to be educators? Edrene is a now retired principal from The Toledo Public Schools and James earned his Ph.D. in Education from Claremont Men's College in California. *Submitted by Edrene Benson Cole, sister of James Russell Benson.*

COUNTER KIDS.

The Red Apple, a short order restaurant and soda fountain, was purchased by Vincent Schwind in 1948. The eatery was located at Central and North Detroit avenues and featured special holiday meals cooked by Mrs. Zelda Schwind for patrons who had no other place to go for holiday fare. The cooks behind the counter are the owner's son-in-law, Romuald Snyder, closest to the camera, and Duane Schwind, the owner's son. *Submitted by Romuald F. Snyder.*

A PUBLIC SERVICE MESSAGE.

Young John Scott reads with members of the Board of Community Relations at WTOL radio studios in 1948. John read the parts for kids in the public service announcements recounting the lives of historical figures. *Submitted by Dr. John Scott.*

OLD BUSINESS.

These Bostwick-Braun Company staffers took a lunch and photo break in 1949. The retail hardware distributor and industrial supplier is one of Toledo's very oldest companies and has operated continuously since it was founded in 1855 as Roff & Company. Brothers, William and Charles B. Roff, sold a successful hardware business in Racine, Wisconsin in order to take advantage of the exploding Toledo market. They were joined by Oscar Alonzo Bostwick in 1862 and Carl F. Braun in 1866. After the founding brothers had retired, the firm changed its name to The Bostwick-Braun Company. *Submitted by, Erica D. Emery, Marketing Manager, The Bostwick-Braun Company.*

A MAN AND HIS CAR.

Robert A. Williams is standing by his car at Michigan and Locust streets. Korman's Grocery is in the background circa 1949. A hero of the time, baseball star, Joe DiMaggio, appears in a Folger's coffee advertisement on the side of the store. *Submitted by Valerie Brazeau, wife of Robert A. Williams nephew.*

A JOB WELL DONE.

Toledo Fire Lieutenant Harry Reed gets a hardy handshake and a big "thank you" for his work of many years with the Old Newsboys Goodfellows Association. Lt. Reed retired after 30 years service with the Toledo Fire Department. *Submitted by Marilyn Reed Dominique, daughgter of Harry Reed.*

ONLY TWO WERE BETTER.

Coach Don Dartt led the Good Shepard School basketball team to third place in the 1949 Catholic Youth Organization (CYO) league. Players in the back row are; (from the left) John Fournier, Roy Brummett, Bob Breisacher, Mike Croak, Bob Steopler, and Tim Croak. Team members in the front row are, from the left: Dick Minarcin, Bob Kline, Jerry Mc Cready, Bob Bowman, and manager Bruce Robinson. *Submitted by David Minarcin, son of Dick Minarcin.*

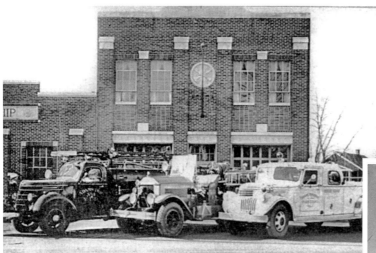

READY TO ROLL.

The Station of the Adams Township Volunteer Fire Department, Company Number 1, is shown here in 1949. The department was organized in 1930 and the station was located on Reynolds Road between Dorr and Bancroft streets. *Submitted by James Tunison, son of former Adam's Township Fire Chief, Harvey Tunison.*

PICNIC BY THE LAKE.

Regina Lee Miller and her daughter, Shirley, enjoy a quiet moment together while picnicking at Toledo Beach during the summer of 1949. *Submitted by Karey Smith, daughter of Shirley Miller Pakulski and granddaughter of Regina Lee Miller.*

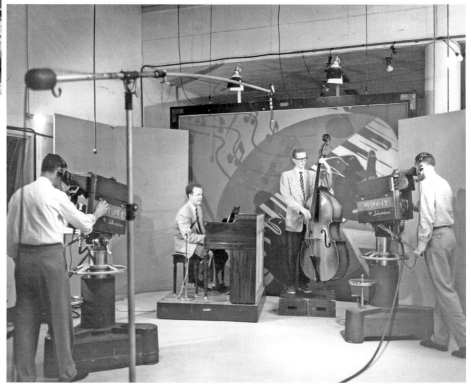

MUSICAL INTERLUDE.

Pianist, El Myers, performs with bassist, Bill Takas, during the breaks of the General Electric Commercial Electric Show on WSPD-TV in 1949. The show highlighted GE products. *Submitted by El Myers.*

Reeb
FUNERAL HOME

For nearly 90 years, Reeb Funeral Home has been conducting business with residents of Northwest Ohio. We have been the choice of thousands of families in their time of need, and have worked diligently to offer caring service at fair prices.

Reeb Funeral Home remains independently owned, operated, and committed, to the same philosophies the business was built on generations ago.

5712 N. Main Street ◆ Sylvania, Ohio
419-882-2033

NOTHING SHADY HERE.

The Dickson brothers arrive at St. Vincent Hospital to install new window shades. Winter, 1950, finds Ernest grabbing the tools, as Marvin unloads the shades. The business continues in Toledo to the present. *Submitted by Karen Lawrence, daughter of Marvin Dickson.*

SHOPPING DAZE.

Seven-year-old Howard Steinman walks alone, heading north, on the west side of Summit Street in 1947. Summit Street was still the heart of downtown retail shopping. Behind Howard are the Lane Drug Company and The Fair Department Store. Directly across the street is Toledo's renowned department store – Tiedtke's. Howard is not far from family, as Jack's Men's Store is just ahead. Jack's was owned by his father, Alvin Steinman, and his grandfather, Jack Steinman (see page 141). *Submitted by Julian Johnsrud.*

BIBLIOGRAPHY

Bend of The River Magazine

The Bulletin of the Green Section of the U.S. Golf Association, January 16, 1922.

Centennial Year In Luckey, Ohio 1881-1981.

Courier & Monroe Ad-Venture

Buchholz, Richard H. *The History of The Old Newsboys Goodfellow Association*, 2000.

Harbaugh, Jack. *Maumee River and Other Toledo Bridges*, 1990.

Inland Seas, Quarterly Journal of the Great Lakes Historical Society, 1958.

Killits, John M., ed. *Toledo and Lucas County, Ohio* 1627-1923, Volume I, 1923.

The Maumee Valley Pioneer Association, *Addresses, Memorials and Sketches*, 1899.

Manufacturing and Mercantile Resources of Toledo, South Toledo, and Perrysburg, 1882.

Mason, John. Letter of February 26, 1985 regarding Ray E. Allen.

McKinney, James P. *The Industrial Advantages of Toledo, Ohio*, 1892.

Mosier-Porter, Tana. *Toledo Profile: A Sesquicentennial History*, 1987.

The Ohio Historical Society

Pot of Gold, Thomas A. DeVilbiss High School, 1933.

Speck, William D. Toledo: *A History of Architecture 1890-1914*, Chicago: Arcadia Publishing, 2002.

Szuch, Yolanda Danyi. *The History of St. Stephen's Church*, 1993.

The Toledo Bee

The Toledo Blade

Toledo City Directories

Toledo History Scrapbooks, The Toledo-Lucas County Public Library.

Toledo Its Motto: Ambition, Perseverance, and Public Spirit, Mercantile Advancement Company, Toledo, Ohio, 1897.

Toledo Monitor

The Toledo News-Bee

Toledo Police Division, 1867-1992, Volume III.

Toledo Sesquicentennial Commission

The Toledo Sunday Journal

The Toledo Times

United States Federal Census

www.oldrhinebeck.org (Baker Electric)

CAPTION WRITERS

Dewayne Todd Archie
Tim Boaden
Ken Dickson
David Eby
Fred Folger
John R. Husman

Ken Levin
Ron Mauter
Kelly J. Norwood
Rolf Scheidel
Jane Bryan Welborn
Sara E. Welborn

EDWIN L. ZEIGIN

at home, 722 Michigan Street on August 5, 1894. He was nine years old. *Photo courtesy of Toledo-Lucas County Public Library. Photographer: Cleo Keller.*

INDEX OF LOCAL AND HISTORICAL SURNAMES

SUBMITTERS OF PHOTOGRAPHS

Marjorie Achinger
Margie Ainsworth
John Binns Albright
Charles D. and Elinor W. Allen
Pat Anaszewicz
Millicent M. Apardian
Dewayne Todd Archie
Carol Ardner
Paula Deatrick Ashton
Martha Curtis Ball
Ann Marie Rizzo Banas
Calvin Banks, Sr.
Larry Barhite
Delbert R. Barhite
Matthew Beach
Bobbi Beagle
Beverly Beasley
Dale F. Beaudry
Jeanne Belding
Lisa Binkowski
Stephen Binkowski
Danita Binkowski
Mary Ann Binkowski
Blade, The
James Blum
Rosmarie Bohnsack
Lori Gurcsik Bolone
Dan Bosch
Bostwick-Braun Company, The
Christine Mather Bothe
Valerie Brazeau
Florence Hamilton Brown
Donald Brown
Deena Georgevich Brueshaber
Richard H. Buckholtz
Rick Bunge
Edna and Donald R. Burwell, Sr.
Carolyn Cahoo
Patt Camp

Helen Hampton Campbell
Rita Roth Cark
Barbara Carr
Jean Carroll
Jean Christy
Annie Cieslukowski
Betty Provo Cochran
Edrene Benson Cole
Bertha Coley
John Connors
Nancy Cooley
Larry and Carol Cousino
Joseph Coyle
Dan Crots
Mike Crowder
Marnette L. Cunningham
Dale-Riggs Funeral Home, Inc.
Alan Davis
Davis College
Salud Gonzalez De Cortez
Glenn DeGelnor
Donna DeVerna
Suzanne Dial
Dean C. Dieball
Doug Dinnebiel
Marilyn Reed Dominique
Bill and Shirley Douge
Howard Drager
Madeline Larberg Drozdowicz
Daniel Drzewiecki
James C. Dunn
David Eby
Fanny Effler
Ella P. Stewart Collection, Center for Archival Collections, B.G.S.U.
Julie Ellison
Erica D. Emery
Norma Ashmann Ethington

Viola Fabian
Marcia Feder-Knorek
Margaret Fern
Richard Fern
Mary J. Finch
Greg Fish
Marian R. Fisher
Jerry Flahie
Emily Fluhrer
Fred Folger
Katherine Franklin
Fr. Dan Fraser
Linda Fravel
Frederick Douglass Community Assoc.
Lee Gagle
Eleanor Gaisser
William Garbe
Mary Beth Schramm Garbe
Charles James Gillespie, Jr.
Patricia Gladfelter
Ross Goodfellow
Joe Gross
Christine Grzochowiak
Lorna Hyott Haines
Margaret M. Hartford
Fred Hepner
Jack Hiles
Ralph Hinkleman
Constance Hoffman
Harold Hoffman
Betty Holub
Peggy Huner
Carolyn Husen
John R. Husman
Richard Ingalsbe
Jeff Jaffe
Dorothy Johansen
Doris Johns
Gloria D. Johnston
Julian Johnsrud
Dennis M. Keesee Collection

Mark Keil
Mary Angela Keller
Tatiana Kirdahy
Tony Kirdahy
Larry and Mary Alice Kish
Dorothy and Joseph Kovesdi
Ron Kozina
Robert Kreiger, Jr.
Kevin Kubiak
Bill LaPountney
Nelle Larson
Veronica Lawrence
Karen Lawrence
Ken Levin
Ruth Lewandowski
Betty Lloyd
Cynthia Mehlow Machnicki
Judy Manders
Michelle H. Marciniak
Mike Marciniak
Christine Martin
Sandra Mattier
Maumee Valley Historical Society
Ron Mauter
Carolyn Mavis
Winifred McBeth
Jerry Melchior
James Meredith
Art Merrill
Miakonda Scouting Museum, Erie Shores Council, Boy Scouts of America
Karen Miller
David Minarcin
Joseph "Louis" Molnar
Shirley Holder Montague
Joan E. Moomey
Jerry Moore
Daisy Gable Moore
Susan Morel

Robert Morris
Patricia P. Munger
El Myers
Giroma Nera
Theresa Nesbitt
Elaine Nicolaidis
Don Noethen
Fr. Richard Notter
Evelyn Nowak
Tim O'Connell
Old Newsboys Goodfellows Assocation, The
Doris Ott
Sandy Owen
Carolyn Owens
Dorothy Pakulski
Shirley Miller Pakulski
Walter Palicki
Tom Parker
Shirley Pawlowski
Ann Fabiszak Payne
Bonnie Peer
Christine Pietrykowski
Mary Lou Pifer
Postmaster, Toledo, Ohio (USPS)
Patricia Presser
Marianne H. Quellhorst
Carolyn Quennan
Sandra Smith Reams
Paul Reheldt
Mary Pat Carter Reifsnider
Jack Reilly
Shirley Reynolds
Sheryl A. Riggs
David Roberts
Doris Roberts
Craig D. Roberts
Anthony Rodriguez
Philip Roth
Roulet Company, The
Richard Royce
Gregory and Patricia Rumer

Suzanne St. John
St. Paul's Lutheran Church
Saints Peter and Paul Catholic Church
Amy Sanislo
Bernard H. Sartor
Marjorie Scalia
Dorothy Schabeck
Rolf Scheidel
William Schoof, Jr.
Dick Schroeder
Leonard Schultz
Janet Scott
Dr. John Scott
Becky Sebring-Huerta
Ed Shabnow
Susan Shaneck
Judy Lebowsky Shook
Ginny Smith
Vivian M. Snyder
Romuald F. Snyder
Hollis Sobb
Mary Kay Solt
Charles Stahl
Florence Stemen
Nancy Stonerock
Kathryn Strand
Roland Strauss
William A. Suder
Joann Dusseau Swanger
Taylor Family
Nancy Zientata Thabit
George Thabit
Katherine Franklin
Third Baptist Church
Jerry Throne
Mary Ann Thurber
Toledo Area Regional Transit Authority (TARTA)
Toledo Firefighters Museum
Toledo Mud Hens Baseball Club

The Toledo-Lucas County Public Library
Toledo Police Department
Carlene Trost
Iris Trzcinski
Judy Johnson Tunison
James Tunison
Mea Vendt
Thomas Vines, Jr.
Louis Visi
Nancy Vuketich
Jean Wagoner
Virginia J. Wagoner
Ann Wajer
Mark Walczak
Walter Funeral Home
Bonna Weaver
Ann Weber
James M. Weislak
Marie Wenzlick
Stephen Werkman
Gary Westfall
Tammy Wheeler
Marilyn Post Wiley
Carmen Williamson
Donald and Arlene Wines
Paul Wirwick, Jr.
Woodlawn Cemetery Assocation
Bob and Karen Woods
Alan and Robin Woody
Elaine Schroeder Wright
Bill Wyatt
Nancy Wynn Hinds
Sharon Yaros
Al Yeager
Daryl Yourist
Roman H. Zawodni
Diane Widmer Zenk
Carol Bauer Zilba
Olive Hyott Zilba

white Family
DEALERSHIPS
A tradition of quality, value, and service since 1914

Founder
Hugh White

*H*ugh White started life as a penniless orphan and by the time he died in 1975 at age 90, he had established one of the largest chains of automobiles in the country.

The White Family Dealers began in 1914 with Hugh White's first Chevrolet store in Zanesville, Ohio. Following his father's example, son Jim White began his dealership in 1940 in Toledo.

Today, Dave White, Sr., Dave White, Jr., Jim White, Jr., Tim White, Sr., and his son, Tim White, Jr., have continued it's founders policy of providing customers with the best purchase and ownership experience as possible.

Twelve dealerships and 26 franchises continue to operate throughout Ohio and parts of Wyoming.

Dave White, Jr.

Dave White, Sr.

Jim White, Jr.

Tim White

Dave White Chevrolet • Dave White Acura
Jim White Honda • Jim White Toyota/Scion • Lexus of Toledo
Hugh White Honda, Columbus
White-Allen Honda • White-Allen Chevrolet/Oldsmobile/Subaru, Dayton
White-Allen European Group Porche/Jaguar/Volkswagen/Audi, Dayton
White's Mountain Motors Chevrolet/Hummer/Subaru, Wyoming
White-Davis Chevrolet/Pontiac/Buick/Cadillac/GMC/Chrysler, Wyoming